CLOSE
ENCOUNTERS
OF THE

KIND

ALSO BY BRIAN GARI:

We Bombed In New London —
The Inside Story of the Broadway Musical Late Nite Comic

A Funny Thing Happened On the Way To My Stress Test

Published in the USA by:
BearManor Media
PO Box 1129
Duncan, Oklahoma 73534-1129
www.bearmanormedia.com

ISBN 978-1-59393-739-3

Printed in the United States of America.

CLOSE
ENCOUNTERS
OF THE
CELEBRITY
KIND

BRIAN GARI

TABLE OF CONTENTS

A big thank you to my mom for being my official editor and for helping to create the title of this book.

Special thanks to Dean Torrence and Sharyn Felder.

Dedicated to my sweet wife Jeanne, for always listening to my stories — even when I start working at six in the morning.

My heartfelt thanks to Ben Ohmart for his continued belief in my writing, the deepest appreciation to Michelle Morgan for introducing me to my wonderful UK editor, Wendy Finn, and to Brian Pearce for his incredible creativity and craftsmanship.

Photographs from the Brian Gari Archives, Dean Torrence, Judy Orbach, and Sharyn Felder.

PREFACE

The cover of this book gives you a glimpse into what the stories will be like. Yes, that's me with Jack Benny on February 27, 1962, when I had just turned ten. I recall listening to "Johnny Jingo" by Hayley Mills (my heartthrob) on the radio, as I put on my black suit and bow tie for the swanky event at the Waldorf Astoria Hotel here in New York City. I was to receive the city's Bronze Medallion on behalf of my grandfather — which I still have — because he was too ill to attend the event.

Left: *"Johnny Jingo" single by Ms. Mills.* Right: *New York City's Bronze Medallion, awarded to my grandfather.*

I remember further back to five years earlier when, on February 10, 1957, the whole family was flown to Miami to the Fontainebleau Hotel, where my grandfather was to celebrate his sixty-fifth birthday (and I, my fifth). He was to be honored for his work on behalf of the State of Israel Bonds. Celebrities included former President Harry S. Truman and my grandfather's close friend Jimmy Durante. February 10 was also Jimmy's birthday, and since mine was on February 18, the band honored us with songs appropriate for each other. My choice was "Popeye the Sailor Man!"

It was a dazzling time for this soon-to-be five-year-old. I was taught to swim by none other than Shelley Winters and danced on the ballroom floor with her daughter, Vittoria (Tordi) Gassman, whose birthday was February 14 — a year, almost to the day, younger than I. She is now a doctor!

There were other brief glimpses into the celebrity arena, such as seeing Merv Griffin at my aunt Marilyn's apartment at 145 West Fifty-Fifth Street. This must have been the late '50s, and, as it turns out, he was a very close family friend for quite a while, having introduced my uncle Robert

Above: *Tordi, my sister Amanda, and me, with Shelley, and my mother.* Right: *Dancing with Tordi Gassman.*

Clary (yes, LeBeau on *Hogan's Heroes*) to my aunt Natalie, resulting in their marriage in 1965. (More on Robert in his chapter.)

I also enjoyed parties at my aunt Edna's beach house at 22050 Pacific Coast Highway in Malibu. It was there that I met great writers like Cy Howard, writer and producer of *My Friend Irma*, and Stewart Stern, writer of *Rebel Without a Cause*. Oh, if only I had been a little older to be able to appreciate and interact with that talented man.

However, I think my biggest thrill was meeting Carl Betz (Dr. Alex Stone on *Donna Reed*) when he dropped by. For this kid, *The Donna Reed Show* was my favorite and had a huge influence on my life. It was on that show that great songs were born ("Johnny Angel" and "My Dad"), sung by cast members Shelley Fabares and Paul Petersen respectively. In recent years, it has come full circle for me, having played piano on "My Dad" for Paul himself in many a venue, including the *Donna Reed Show* Season 3 DVD.

I vaguely remember being at NBC for the *Jack Paar Tonight Show* in 1958 or 1959. They had a segment called *It's All Relative*, where Paar had to guess the famous person you were related to, and somehow my sister (age four) and I were the mystery guests. I ran into Dick Cavett some years later, who told me that was his segment to produce and that he may well have met me back then. For me, the excitement was meeting

Robert with Merv at piano, early '50s.

Charley Weaver (Cliff Arquette). He was an idol of mine, so much so that I actually dressed up as him in a home movie. I wish so much that this videotape of the television segment would show up somewhere.

In the '70s, I had brief encounters that I wish were detailed enough for chapters, but alas, they aren't. In my travels as a songwriter, I met with Tony Orlando, who took a straight job as a publisher before "Tie a

Left: *Dressing up as Charley Weaver, circa 1960.* Above: *My high school diploma was signed by James Earl Jones!*

Yellow Ribbon" was a hit. He was very kind to me in that position. I also met with Lloyd Price of "Personality" fame. He was an A&R man (artists and repertoire) looking for songs. We chatted about his cousin, the late Larry Williams, who, Lloyd told me, couldn't decide whether he wanted to be a hit songwriter and artist ("Bony Moronie," "Short Fat Fannie," "Slow Down," "Dizzy Miss Lizzie," and "Bad Boy") or a pimp! I also had a wonderful meeting with Broadway songwriter Stephen Schwartz, before his huge success with shows like *Wicked, Godspell,* and *Pippin.*

And of all things, my high school diploma was signed by none other than James Earl Jones!

So there you have it. This will be a journey into my funny, sad, nasty, and thrilling encounters with celebrities. Hope you enjoy the trip.

Brian Gari
Summer 2013
New York City

EDDIE CANTOR

I certainly could not write a book about the celebrities I've known without including Eddie. I was fortunate to get to know my grandfather for the first twelve years of my life. It wasn't for quite a while that I realized what a huge star he was.

He was number one in every facet of the entertainment industry: starting out in vaudeville; appearing in *Florenz Ziegfeld's Follies*; breaking all records at the Palace; and, finally, having his name above the title in the book show *Whoopee*. Speaking of records, he made plenty of them: scoring smash hits for Victor, Columbia, Decca, and many other labels. Those hits included "Makin' Whoopee," "If You Knew Susie," "Ida," and "Margie." He went on to radio, starring in the number one show for many years and introducing songs like "Santa Claus Is Comin' To Town" and "Try a Little Tenderness." He even wrote a song called "Merrily We Roll Along," which became the Merrie Melodies cartoon theme — one of the most memorable tunes ever written!

His films were enormous box office hits. Some of the titles were *Whoopee*, *Palmy Days*, *Kid Millions*, *Roman Scandals*, and *The Kid From Spain*. When these films first aired on television in the early '60s, my mother would wake up my sister and me to watch them on the *Late, Late Show*. Though a little bleary eyed, we had a very enjoyable time.

As part of his philosophy of living, he also "gave back a lot" with his charitable efforts, such as starting The March of Dimes. He did benefit after benefit during the war, to help wounded soldiers and to get men, women, and children out of their dangerous surroundings overseas. He gave large sums from his own pocket. When television arrived, Eddie Cantor was the only host of the *Colgate Comedy Hour* to beat *Ed Sullivan* every time in the ratings. (And they were good friends!) It was at this time in his life that I came along.

My grandfather visited New York (my home) from California (his final residence) only a few more times after his heart attack in 1952. He hosted the *Colgate Comedy Hour* from California in 1951, after his first season in New York. He continued doing that and his radio shows until the mid-1950s.

I started making trips with my family to the West Coast at a very early age. When I started school, we would end up spending every summer out there. It was a ball! As I mentioned, I really didn't know I had a famous grandfather; I just knew he was a lot of fun. He tried out his old vaudeville magic tricks on me, like making a banana go from ear-to-ear or turn into a quarter. He had a captive audience in me — and a good laugher as well.

Here I am in 1954 with my grandpa and grandma.

His big trademark eyes were full of joy, and his hair was as black as shoe polish — which he was probably using on it at the time.

We had great times together. I used to love to watch cartoons at his house because NBC had given him one of the first color TVs. What an event that was for me to see my animated friends in living color — a far cry from my tiny black-and-white set in New York. I'll never forget a particular lunch and movie with him: He asked what film I would like to see, and I mentioned the Three Stooges' new one called *Have Rocket Will Travel*. Well, I couldn't have found a more perfect movie for grandpa and grandson — they were old friends of his! We went into Beverly Hills to have lunch — which was a cheeseburger and a milkshake — and then to Hollywood for the movie. I was only seven years old.

My grandfather didn't have a swimming pool at his last home, but he didn't want his grandkids to miss out on one of the summer joys of a California trip. He instead called his friends — Groucho Marx, Dinah Shore, and songwriter Jimmy McHugh — and sent my mother and her kids off to their houses for a day of swimming. This was such a different lifestyle compared to my city escapades. In fact, it was similar in a way to my grandfather's experience as a kid. He only knew the streets of New York, but was given a chance to see the countryside when he was sent by the Educational Alliance of New York City to Surprise Lake Camp for two weeks. He said he had never seen that much green except on a pool table, and he supported the Camp for the rest of his life.

Although there were sweet memories of my grandfather (and grandmother, Ida), there were also sad memories. He had to have an oxygen

---

```
                    EDDIE CANTOR


                    June 8th, 1964


      Dear Dear Brian,


                    What a thrill to receive
      your letter of June 3rd.      And what a thrill
      to hear that you are doing so well in school!
      You may not believe it, but these days, you
      can't get enough education, nor work hard enough
      at it, regardless of what field you are going
      into when you grow up.


                    I want to congratulate you
      on your organizational ability with the CAT CLUB
      and collecting dues, etc.    It's really a worthy
      cause and I'm so proud of you.


                    I can hardly wait to see
      either you or the movies you've produced.
      From all appearances, it seems to me, you'll be
      the one to carry on the tradition of Show Business
      in the family.


                    And to think of your winning
      ten dollars at the tv shows!   How about a loan,
      kid.


                    I am doing my best to get in
      better shape so that we can have more fun together
      when you arrive.


                    Until then -- all my love --


                         Grandpa
```

Grandpa's final letter to me.

unit in his bedroom to help him through his later years. His first daughter, Margie, passed away from cancer at the age of forty-four in 1959. Ida died in 1962. These deaths really took their toll on my grandfather. He finally passed away in 1964.

His final letter to me from June of that year was ironic. He said he felt I would be the one to carry on the show business tradition in the family. Well, not only did I write all the songs for a musical that ended up on Broadway but it was also I who produced all the CDs, tapes, and DVDs featuring Eddie Cantor that are currently available on the market. I am so proud of preserving his work. Not only that, but a fan letter came in from a lady asking if she could start a fan club in memory of my grandfather. It couldn't have been more perfect timing. The fan club was established in 1993 by Sheila Riddle and passed over to Michelle Malik a few years later; the membership has been growing ever since. Hopefully, with all of these products and a character (albeit a phonied-up one) on HBO's *Boardwalk Empire*, my grandfather will never be forgotten.

DANNY THOMAS

I think it was 1963, and I was eleven years old, when I went out to California for our annual family summer visit to see my grandparents, aunts, and cousins. It was always a wonderful time — except for the forced summer reading I had to do for the all-boys school I went to in Manhattan. The books were mostly boring and killed my interest in reading until much later in life. Now I can't stop.

One of my favorite shows on television was *The Danny Thomas Show*; my grandfather got wind of this fact and called his buddy — Danny Thomas! He made arrangements for me and my sister to actually visit the set of the show, meet the cast, and watch an episode being filmed. I wish I could say I recall the particular episode, but alas I cannot. I do recall going over to Desilu and encountering the late Rusty Hamer, who played Danny's son and was five years older than I was. He was in the middle of shining his shoes and was not particularly friendly. I had a major crush on Angela Cartwright, but I don't remember any interaction with her, or any other members of the cast for that matter. Oh yes, Pat Carroll was a good friend of the family at that time, and she was great. The filming was fascinating, and I had a wonderful time.

A year later, as my grandfather's health worsened, Danny Thomas often visited him to share stories and reminisce. He really stood by him. Which brings me to the meat of this story, and something that totally confused me about this guy…

Jump to 1973 when I saw Mr. Thomas sing a song on *Johnny Carson*. It was an original song entitled "The Best Thing That Ever Happened To Me," written by Jim Weatherly. Yes, the same song that became a hit for Gladys Knight & the Pips later that year. I was twenty-one years old and trying to get my songs recorded by anyone. In those days, a credit was a credit, and there was always a possibility that an "old timer" might get a hit — or at least a spot on national television that might bring in a few bucks. So I contacted Roz Starr, who was quite well known here in the New York area for her weekly sheet that showed you who was in town and where they were staying. It seemed Mr. Thomas was in New

York and staying at some swanky hotel on Central Park South. I gathered up my courage, called the hotel, and asked to be connected to him. Of course, you had to guess the right time to call, as you didn't want to wake somebody if it was too early and you didn't want to miss them if you waited too long. I think I called around noon, and he answered the phone!

I said, "Hello Mr. Thomas. My name is Brian Gari and my grandfather was Eddie Cantor. How are you?" (I normally did not use my grandfather's name to open doors, but in this case it truly made sense.)

He responded, "I've got a fuckin' earache."

Hmmm. Great response. Now what do I do?

"I'm so sorry, Mr. Thomas," I continued. "I saw you sing on *Johnny Carson* and I was wondering if you would consider one of my songs?"

He paused and asked, "Is it published?"

I proudly answered, "Yes, Mr. Thomas!"

He gruffly retorted, "Then I'm not interested. I only sing songs I publish!"

With that, he hung up the phone. So much for my Cantor connections. It turns out "The Best Thing That Ever Happened To Me" was owned and published by Keca Music — Danny Thomas's publishing company.

Danny Thomas second from left, Eddie Cantor third from right, at Thomas's closing at the Copa NYC, January 17, 1951.

JOHN LENNON

It was Saturday, February 8, 1964, and the Beatles had arrived at JFK the day before. Word quickly spread that they were staying at the Plaza Hotel. Armed with my 8mm Kodak movie camera — which was stolen two years later — I went with my sister to see if we could meet the Beatles (good album title.) I was almost twelve years old and smack in the middle of the British Invasion and Beatlemania. The Top Ten was already featuring "I Want To Hold Your Hand," on Capitol, and "She Loves You," on Swan. I had both 45s with their picture sleeves and couldn't stop playing them. So it was natural that if they were in my city, I should make my way over to Fifth Avenue and Fifty-Ninth Street to see them.

Of course, it was already a mob scene. The screaming fans were absolutely frantic, but there were protesters as well. They were holding signs

One of the many protesters in front of the Plaza that day

like "I Wanna Cut Your Hair," "Ban the Bugs" (featuring a can of Raid), and "Beetles Can't Spell Goode." Those guys had crew cuts.

We had a false alarm when a convertible passed by and four guys with wigs waved at us. But the real deal did come along, and I ran with the others to catch a glimpse of the Fab Four. I think they were on their way to a rehearsal for their *Ed Sullivan* debut the next night. I kept my

The back of a Beatles' head in the limo.

camera running and actually caught a frame of the back of one of their heads. Cheap home movie cameras were not automatic for lighting back then, and the limo was dark, so I got what I got and was grateful. I bet you're wondering if I still have the film: of course I do!

By 1977, the Beatles had broken up and they were making solo albums. I was exhibiting my musical skills as a performer, sandwiched in between comedians at the Comic Strip comedy club on Second Avenue between Eighty-First and Eighty-Second Street. I had started to work with various singers at the club, and one such performer was Robin Kaiser. In developing a night club act for her, I was able to intersperse some of my favorite known tunes into the mix. One such song was "I'll Be Back," from the *Beatles '65* album. I had always loved that song by the Beatles as well as by Roger Nichols and the Small Circle of Friends. It was a very pretty song, and I must say Robin and I had a very nice arrangement of it.

One night, when I stepped outside to take a break from the endless lineups of comedians and jokes, I looked up Second Avenue, and saw John Lennon himself approaching. I was shocked to see this icon sporting a cap and walking toward me with a friend of his. I didn't know what to do or say. Obviously, there was no need to do anything, but I simply had to respond. So I blurted out, "Hi John, we're doing one of your songs inside." He was very nice, gave me a nod and a thank you, and kept walking. It wasn't until I thought about what had just happened that I realized what I said was one of the dopiest things I could have ever uttered to the bloke. We're doing one of his songs? Like he was a desperate songwriter, hoping and praying that someone like Brian Gari would cover him. Like no one else had ever done a Beatles song. Oh, screw it. I got to meet John Lennon.

LITTLE RICHARD, DICK CLARK, AND AMERICAN BANDSTAND

I had no clue that the Summer of 1964 was to be my last summer visiting California for years to come; it turned out my grandfather had just four months to live. His passing would mean the end of annual family visits to this idyllic environment. Well, at least to a twelve-year-old. My sister took it to heart and relocated there years later, not realizing, I'm sure, that the place was not what it used to be, and you had to have a car and lots of money for gas!

I recall my mother driving us kids down Pico Boulevard to the newly constructed May Company department store, where I carved my name into the fresh cement near the store. (I wonder if it's still there?) Upon spying a small record store across the street, I stopped in and purchased — for 77¢ — a picture sleeve 45 of Jan & Dean singing "The Little Old Lady (From Pasadena)." You couldn't get more California than that. Do I still have the 45? Of course I do!

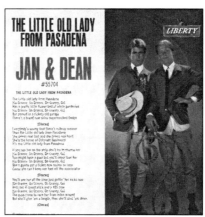

"The Little Old Lady (From Pasadena)."

My cousin Mike was working over at ABC as a producer/writer for Chuck Barris — doing *The Dating Game* and *Newlywed Game* shows — and he would run into Dick Clark, as Clark was now doing *American Bandstand* in California after a long run in Philadelphia. Clark had seen some of my cousin's collage art and asked him to do one on him. The only request: don't use pictures of me with my old hair style.

23

I was a typical twelve-year-old; I was into rock and roll and watching all the shows that featured that music. So you can imagine my excitement when my cousin offered to get me into *American Bandstand* one Saturday — despite the fact I was actually underage. I could also invite a dancing partner. Now, keep in mind, I had been attending an all-boys school, and the amount of dancing was limited to the moronic dance parties organized for the mostly homosexual school when they'd import females from the all-female schools in the area. It was very awkward, and all it got me was my 45s having my name written all over them so they could return them to me after being played at the dance.

I called my childhood sweetheart, Cindy, and asked her to the show. She accepted very gladly. The funny thing was, she was quite tall at almost thirteen years old, probably close to five feet ten

My childhood sweetheart, Cindy,

inches, and I was not full grown — I was a lot shorter at that time. It didn't matter to me.

We were driven by Cindy's mother to the ABC studios on July 22, to tape three one-hour-long shows. The Prospect Studios was named as such because it was at 4151 Prospect Avenue in the Los Feliz section of Los Angeles, just east of Hollywood. It had been built in 1915 as the Vitagraph Studios, and when Warner Brothers took it over in 1927, they filmed portions of *The Jazz Singer* there. ABC took it over in 1948, and by 1964, the *Lawrence Welk Show* as well as many other shows, were being taped there. It was later home to numerous ABC sitcoms.

Out of the three shows being taped that day, one was an all-Beatles show, featuring only their music and no guests. The other shows included the acts Rene and Rene, the Premieres, Dale & Grace, and the iconic Little Richard.

I was more savvy than most twelve-year-olds, and I knew everything about Little Richard, even though he had been more important in the '50s. Little Richard was born Richard Penniman, and I came to know his work through Paul McCartney screaming his "Long Tall Sally" on the Beatles' Second Album. I actually sought out all writers of the songs I enjoyed, to find out where the original versions came from. When the writing credit of Richard Penniman appeared, I found out that was the real name of Little Richard, and I bought his first album on Specialty. These albums cost this kid a little more than the current hits, as they weren't on a major label and they were a bit obscure — inasmuch as the music biz eats you up and spits you out in a fairly short amount of time.

Getting Little Richard's autograph on Bandstand, *July 1964.*

Cindy and I danced away on the Bandstand floor. I was wearing a white shirt, black tie, and red sweater — yes, there were actually dress codes for the show. Songs by acts like Patience and Prudence — who I produced a CD for, decades later — were playing, as we did "the slop" and "mashed potatoes." One of the features of the show was a stop at the autograph table, to get the autographs of the acts signed on official *American Bandstand* stationery — remember this moment as I will have a great story about it later.

I got the autographs of a few of the lesser-known acts, but my thrill was to get in line for Little Richard. I stood behind the older kids — who were actually teenagers — as I waited for my grand moment with the King of Rock and Roll. Just as I said the words to Richard for my autograph, "To Brian…," Richard was interrupted by Dick Clark, who had come over to chat while the music was playing. I was devastated. I thought I had lost my chance. Not so. But it sure looked and felt that way. Do I still have that autograph? Of course I do! In fact, I got to tell Richard this story when I met him at *Live! With Regis & Kathie Lee* in the '90s. He autographed his book for me.

There is a wonderful footnote to this story. On June 6, 1990, I was asked to accept an award on behalf of my grandfather for his work in radio on the show *Take It Or Leave It*. He had been one of five different hosts taking over in 1949 through 1950. The event was at the Plaza Hotel, and I was there with Alan Colmes, Allison Steele, Charles Osgood, Frank Stanton, Paul Harvey, Pete Fornatale, and yes, Dick Clark. Howard Stern's clan was there to sabotage Clark with questions like, "Did you have on any pants when you were behind the podium on *American Bandstand*?" Clark was sort of confused by these types of questions until I whispered to him that it was the work of Howard Stern. Clark was relieved and grateful to me for exposing the culprit.

I told Clark my Bandstand story and mentioned the autographs and a video I had of a 1963 special he had done. Being a major collector himself, he asked if I could possibly find it in my heart to part with one of the autographs on the official Bandstand paper, as he had absolutely none of those in his collection. He also didn't have that 1963 video. I said I would send him both. On a lark, I asked if the tapes of the shows that I appeared on still existed. He asked me to write him with the dates and/or descriptions. I did, and I received a note back telling me he found the shows and he was going to make copies for me. Imagine my thrill when the tapes arrived and I got to go back in time to a wonderful experience with Cindy and the good old days of rock and roll. Thank you, Dick Clark.

At the Emerson Radio Hall of Fame Awards, June 1990.

NEIL SEDAKA

In the spring of 1966, I looked up my idol, Neil Sedaka, in the Manhattan directory. He was listed. It was really his business office, but a connection just the same. I actually typed out a letter and sent it to 756 Seventh Avenue — sadly, the building has been torn down.

In June of the same year, I received a photo postcard that was a hand-written response and forwarded to Westport, Connecticut, the place where we were living that summer. You can imagine how thrilling it was for me. Here I was, a fourteen-year-old fan who lip synched to Sedaka in my mirror, with a handwritten postcard from him in my possession. I knew every word and every move to "Next Door To An Angel." I listened to that song over and over, as I fell asleep with disc jockey Cousin Brucie of WABC spinning it through my tiny red transistor radio, which I kept under my pillow after lights out at 9 p.m. Do I still have that radio? Of course I do! And I bought the record.

The postcard said:

I received your very nice typed letter. So happy you are enjoying my songs and records. Also happy your mother likes my music. I want to wish you the very best in your writing of songs. You seem to know all the good writers. Sorry I do not have a photo of Mr. Greenfield.

Regards, Neil

Do I still have that postcard? Of course I do!

Well, I knew I had to meet this man. I ventured downtown after the summer and simply stopped by the office. It was upstairs in a two- or three-story old building and was filled with files and jammed with papers. An older man let me in, who I now believe was his notorious manager, Ben Sutter. Nothing much was going on, but Neil, dressed in a t-shirt and dress pants, came by for a moment and left just as fast. We didn't really connect. After all, I was quite young and had shown up unannounced with really no business there. However, it was not the last time we would see each other.

In the spring of 1967, Neil had a great song out called "We Had a Good Thing Goin'" recorded by the Cyrkle. I had seen it performed on the *Clay Cole Show*. Strangely enough, Neil performed it on Cousin Brucie's show *Go Go* a half an hour later — but his version was impossible to find! Why? Because, when I called the station, they told me it was his "demo." Yes, an unreleased version that was shown to the Cyrkle to record. My mission was to find this recording.

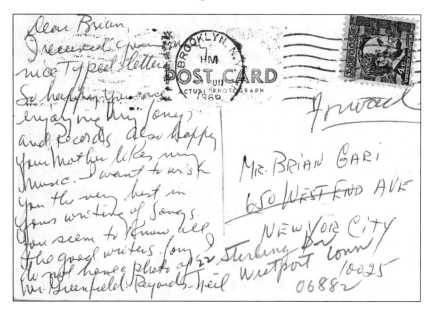

Above: My first connection with Neil. Left: My original red transistor radio! Right: The original demo disc I paid $5 for!

At about the same time, I was showing my songs to the Tokens at 1697 Broadway, and their musical director, Norman Bergen, played me another great Sedaka song they were doing with the Chiffons called "Teach Me How." It was Neil singing and playing only the piano on yet another unreleased song. I had to have it. I was directed to the publisher.

When I called Screen Gems Music, they told me the only way to get a copy was to call the recording studio, Dick Charles. I did just that, and they told me I would have to pay $3.50. $3.50???? That was a lot for a 15-year-old — especially for one song! They said I also might as well get one more song for the other side, as it would then only be a total of $5. Of course, I also wanted that song by the Cyrkle, so I went for it. I practically wore out the disc — they're not meant to be played more than a few times. Do I still have that disc? Of course I do!

In the meantime, my mother had a lead on Sedaka's contact info. She had a friend who knew his dentist. She called him and got his number. I gathered up the courage to call, and Neil answered. He was very nice and said we could get together at his publisher, Screen Gems.

I was so excited about being able to meet my idol. It was at 711 Fifth Avenue on the eighth floor — the home of Screen Gems Columbia Music. Since it was summer, Neil was once again in casual clothes. He greeted me warmly, showed me around the offices, and introduced me to his longtime writing partner, Howard Greenfield, who was another nice man. Neil and Howie were working on a song that eventually came out, called "Rainy Jane" by Davy Jones. In fact, Neil came rushing out of the office humming a part that he felt reminded him of another song. I told him it was a Petula Clark tune. He immediately went back in and changed one note.

Then he came out again and asked me if I'd like to meet any other writers. I mentioned Carole King, but Neil said she didn't come up there very often. I then asked about Helen Miller (she had written "Foolish Little Girl" among so many others), and he pointed her out as she was coming up the hallway. I asked if she was Helen Miller, and she responded with, "Who the fuck wants to know?" I later found out Helen had quite a mouth and was very funny. We were friends right up to the end of her life.

Neil then asked if I wanted any of the demos he made. This was like Christmas in July! I responded in the affirmative, and he directed me to the demo file cabinets. I could take anything and as much as I wanted. Keep in mind, these are the same discs that I would have had to pay $3.50 for!

It wasn't over yet. There was a gated area where they kept the 45 RPM records of the songs that were already released. I could raid that as well! I packed up quite a load. Some even had picture sleeves.

Neil then listened to some of my early songs and brought me right in to Al Altman, the professional manager. Neil recommended they sign me. It didn't happen. I think I was a little too young.

As I left, I thanked him profusely and asked if he and his wife would like to come to dinner sometime. He said yes and that I should call him.

I left with my goodie bag of records and went straight to my father's house for dinner — my parents were separated by that time. I loaded up his record player with all these Sedaka recordings, and drove him nuts as the records never stopped coming.

My mother, ever the brilliant hostess, was pleased that Neil and his wife, Leba, would want to come to dinner. She immediately put together a wonderful guest list, which included composer Arthur Siegel and author Sandford Dody. We called Neil and Leba, and they were delighted to accept the invitation. It all happened in the winter, and Neil showed up in a white suit. He immediately went over to the piano and played most of the night — he loved it. I requested so many of his great songs, and he also played some new ones. I recall "One More Ride On the Merry-Go-Round," which got recorded by Peggy Lee. He also did a song the Chiffons cut, called "Lucky Me," which pleased my mother greatly as she loved that melody, particularly the bridge.

Neil was enthralled with our other guests, especially Sandy Dody. Sandy was always so gregarious, and Neil was very much impressed. He even brought along a photo of himself in blackface doing an Eddie Cantor salute from his act. Do I still have that photo? Of course I do!

Can you imagine — we even got a thank you note from Leba, who emphasized that she wanted us to be their guests at a party in their home in Brooklyn. I couldn't believe it — I was going to Neil Sedaka's house for a party!

I can't recall how we got to Brooklyn — it might have been the subway, as a cab would have been way too expensive. When we got there, Neil said he was sorry but Connie couldn't make it — yes, he meant Connie Francis. However, there was Cousin Brucie, Lesley Gore, Howard Greenfield, and Carole Bayer (before she became Sager.) Bobby Vinton may also have been there. They showed us around their huge apartment — it was actually two, the wall between having been torn down to connect them both. There was a grand piano on a platform in the living room, where everyone sang oldies — both Sedaka's and others. Then we got the grand tour. That included the bedroom, which featured — are you ready? — a heart-shaped bed! The party was so much fun. I can't recall what we ate, but I do recall his daughter, Dara, singing "Born Free" — and quite well, I may add. She eventually had some success as a singer — and should have been a bigger success in my opinion.

Above: *Sedaka in blackface as Cantor.* Below: *Leba Sedaka's thank you note.*

Neil and Leba came by for more parties over the next year, but, eventually, the Sedakas moved to England and we lost touch — though not forever.

Jump to 2003 when I was given the assignment of writing the book for a box set for a German company called Bear Family. They were going to release everything on Neil from 1956 to 1966, and who better for the job

Friars Club

Salutes

Neil Sedaka

Joy Behar
Mistress of Ceremonies

Monday, March 31, 2003
Cocktails & Dinner
6:00 - 8:00 PM

Show
9:00 PM

Performers Scheduled to Appear

Dick Fox	Jane Olivor
Brian Gari	Regis Philbin
Kathie-Lee Gifford	Jay Siegel (The Tokens)
Leslie Gore	Stewie Stone
Billy Stritch	

Accompanists
Tim Ditchel, Barry Levitt, Chris Marlowe, Tracy Stark, Carl Vreeland

than I. That would also mean getting back in touch with Neil, who couldn't have been more receptive.

I came up to their place on Park Avenue and took a tour of their new home. Just fantastic. I also brought up some rare recordings and videos that impressed Neil so much. We had such a great time together. I showed him an episode of *I've Got a Secret* from 1965. He pointed out a gorgeous ring he had on, which got stolen when he left it on the piano during a tour.

I asked him if he would like to see me do a salute to him for his birthday in March. He loved the concept, and we set the date for March 12. I worked really hard on this concert. It was just me at the piano and guitar. I did medleys and rare songs and told stories. The thrill for me was when Neil decided to come up at the end of the show and do a song with me. The place went nuts. So did I. So did Neil — so much so, that he asked me to open a Friar's Club show of his music at the end of the month. I opened for Lesley Gore, Jay Siegel of the Tokens, Regis & Kathie Lee, and Jane Olivor.

Neil asked me to repeat my tribute show in June of that same year, which I also did. Again, Neil joined me for an encore.

We then disappeared from each other's lives until the spring of 2012, when I showed up at the Ninety-Second Street Y, where he was doing a seminar. I stood in line with the book to the box set for him to sign. He saw me from afar and was absolutely floored and overjoyed to see me — but noticed how frail I was. This was my first outing after open heart surgery. He and Leba were very concerned. He posed for photos with me and signed my book "Love You So."

I also showed him that first postcard he sent me. He looked at it wistfully and said:

"My father."

"What?" I queried.

"That's my father's handwriting. He used to answer all my fan mail personally."

P.F. Sloan publicity photo, circa 1966.

P.F. SLOAN

The postmark on the large postcard said March 2, 1966. I was barely fourteen years old, but already a confirmed P.F. Sloan fan. He had written some of the biggest songs of the '60s like "Secret Agent Man" (Johnny Rivers) and the classic protest song "Eve of Destruction" (Barry McGuire.) Even his name fascinated me. I knew his real name was Phil, but where did P.F. come from? Easy — Phil and Flip (short for Philip and Flip, his nickname during the surf period when he wrote and sang backup for people like Jan and Dean. He was the high voice on "The Little Old Lady From Pasadena.")

I had his second solo Dunhill album with the shiny paper cover. It seemed unusual in and of itself. Most albums utilized flat, dull paper, but this one almost reflected one's own image in Phil's. I never saw another like it.

The postcard was from Dunhill Records on South Beverly Drive in Beverly Hills, California. I had written there because the second album mentioned I could get a booklet called "The Dunhill Story," featuring artists like Jan & Dean, Johnny Rivers, Shelley Fabares, and Terry Black. It seemed like a dream booklet for a fan like me — and a promotional gimmick for

Left: *My P.F. Sloan period.* Right: *Sloan's second album*

manager and executive Lou Adler. The postcard said they were out of booklets, although, years later, Dean Torrence of Jan & Dean revealed to me that it never existed! Do I still have that postcard? Of course, I do!

But there was something else on this card. A promotional offer of $1 off a list price of $3.98 to get P.F. Sloan's debut album. Since it had been a fluke that I even was able to find the second one — with the razor slash

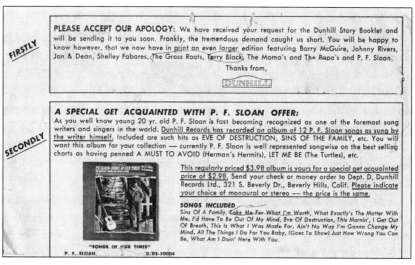

The promotional postcard.

and inked $2.69 price in the lower right hand corner where the Sam Goody record store always marked the price — I decided to send away for the album. The sum of $2.98 was a little more than this 14-year-old wanted to pay, but I somehow knew it would be a long road finding this album anytime soon. The odd part about my whole fascination with Sloan was that I was also seeking his endeavors as a surfing performer, which was in full bloom only a year and a half earlier. Here was an artist with such depth on the Dunhill label, yet only a short time earlier, he was singing about bikinis, woodies, and impersonating Ricky Nelson and Elvis! I didn't care: I loved both sides. If I wanted fluff I could listen to Jan and Dean's lighthearted version of "I Found a Girl," if I wanted introspection, I could listen to Phil's version.

During early 1966, I recall writing to Liberty Records in Hollywood about the Fantastic Baggys album and two rare singles I couldn't find. (Phil and his partner Steve Barri were the Baggys.) I got back a form letter with a typed in addendum — those two singles have been deleted, and you must place the LP on order with the distributor. I was in the ninth grade for God's sake! What did I know about distributors??? Well, I must have known something, because the next thing I knew, I was using my school bus pass to go to the warehouse at 601 West Fiftieth Street — so far west that it was practically in the Hudson River — to a place called Malverne Distributors. I must have looked pretty cute to this one lady when she saw a little boy in a school uniform ready to

LIBERTY RECORDS, INC. 6920 SUNSET BOULEVARD / LOS ANGELES, CALIFORNIA (90028) / PHONE (213) 464-8101 / CABLE: LIBRECORD

66072, 66092 & 66096 have been deleted. As for the two LP's, the order would have to be placed through a dealer with our distributor who would in turn order from us. We cannot arbitrarily send records to any distributor.

Thank You
For Your
Recent Letter

Dear Customer:

We regret that the selection that you inquired about has been deleted from our catalog and is, therefore, no longer available.

In large cities there are usually "rare record shops"-- that is, record shops that specialize in locating hard-to-find records. These shops would be listed in the classified section of the telephone directory, probably under Phonograph Records - Retail.

If there is none in your vicinity, you might write to:

        Ray Avery Rare Records
        415 East Broadway
        Glendale, California

We realize how frustrating it is to want a record that is no longer available and we hope this information will be of help to you.

Very truly yours,

LIBERTY RECORDS, INC.

Carole M. Robinson

Carole M. Robinson
Consumer Relations

P.S. We thought you might like to have copies of our most recent catalogs which you will find enclosed.

LIBERTY · DOLTON · IMPERIAL · WORLD PACIFIC · PACIFIC JAZZ

The letter from Liberty Records.

Steve Barri publicity photo, circa 1966.

plunk down his $4 that he saved up for a month from his allowance for a Fantastic Baggys LP! Imagine how my eyes must have lit up when she simply gave me the album.

My interest in Phil and Steve grew to the point where I had to write them fan letters. Steve responded quickly with an autographed photo and the new P.F. Sloan single! It was called "City Women," which completely knocked me out. I learned the song as fast as I could on my guitar. Now, what other 14-year-old was singing "City Women" — with a voice that hadn't changed yet. Phil wrote me as well, and he enclosed a photo that was inscribed "thanks for being a fan" with a signature that sort of looked as if he was almost going to sign it Phil, but quickly changed his mind and made it "P.F."

It was October 20, 1967, and I was still an avid fan, when I picked up a magazine that was run by Robin Leach called "Go." It was really a publicist's field day, because all it did was feature rock and roll artists and what they were up to, as well as a local radio chart. The magazine was free at your local record store, and I never missed an issue.

While leafing through this mesmerizing fanzine — they were never called that back then — I came across a blurb in Richard Robinson's column that said P.F. Sloan had made the move to New York City recently from the coast. I called "Go" and managed to convince a secretary

Richard Robinson Reporting

PETER LEEDS . . . successful man behind the music business scene.

Spent last Saturday afternoon at The Apollo to catch Arthur Conley's sweet soul act. Arthur was in great form and really wowed the audience. I'd like to say a few words about the whole Apollo approach to music.

First there is a house band that is a groove. They are musicians all the way and they never overpower the performers. Second, the sound system is excellent . . . you can always hear who's singing what. Third, the show starts on time and runs like clock work. No stage waits . . . no filling in . . . just no nonsense whatsoever. (And all this happens with at least five acts on the bill and four or five shows a day!)

The opening act, The Precisions, will be a group that can't help but become a permanent part of the soul scene. Their material is good and their stage act is a departure from the expected. They're using a lot of free form and jazz dance things that are very nice. Check out their first release, "If This Is Love" on Drew Records.

Seems as if Mr. Bonner and Mr. Gordon are on the verge of starting a whole new happy sound. "Happy Together" was a start but between "As Long As You're Here" and "The Heart Of Juliet Jones" there is definitely a new sound happening. I wonder if I can get away with calling it Big Band Spoonful? Anyway, Gary Bonner's first single effort, "The Heart Of Juliet Jones", is perfect.

Who is that peeking over Jerry Yester's shoulder in new Spoonful ads? Could it be...?

Stax/Volt men Sam and Dave heading for Europe and England again for the second time this year. The tour will last a month and will include Arthur Conley and Percy Sledge.

A new happening store opened in New York this week. Variety's Child is a clothes store with an angle—17,000 costumes from past theatrical performances. Everything is for sale (an accumulation of 35 years of show business clothes) and New York area groups have been going wild over the place as has the public. Definitely worth a visit when you're in town.

The Who have just announced a four week tour of the U. S., which they will start on November 15. The tour will take them from Coast to Coast on a series of one-nighters that

my job is to move an act along as soon and as fast as is possible. It is important that a manager sees that his groups are ready for recording commitments and tour bookings. I guess it all comes down to knowing that, if your client isn't making it, it isn't your fault. As a manager you have to be able to live with yourself. Too many people are only looking for money," Peter said.

Peter has come a long way since he first started running dances in New Jersey and it's not hard to see that nothing can stop him from hitting the top.

Sam The Sham stopped to say hello to Eric Burdon and the Animals last week when they were in town. Also, a major magazine came over to do an article on the group. The angle was something about rock 'n' roll groups having sideburns. Unfortunately not all of the Animals have sideburns so the whole article sort of faded. Maybe someday they'll do an article on music.

P.F. Sloan made the move to New York recently from the Coast. Rumour is that Phil will have a group soon.

P.F. Sloan made the move to New York recently from the Coast. Rumour is that Phil will have a group soon.

to reveal where Phil was staying. (A budding stalker?) She told me it was the Chelsea Hotel, so I simply picked up the phone and asked for his room. Lo and behold, he answered. He talked strangely about the pigeons on his window, but consented to come to my house for dinner.

My mother was as adventurous as I and welcomed my interest in associating with songwriters. She also made a great meatloaf — although that night Phil pointed out to her that the bottom was burned. He arrived at my house and went directly to my room with wild eyes and a long Sergeant-Pepper-like trench coat. It was odd that he knew where my room was, as he had never been there before. During dinner he was blunt, but obviously intelligent. He played his guitar and talked about politics and "Elizabeth Taylor's naked backside" in *Reflections In a Golden Eye*. Moments  later, after scribbling a name on the pad near the phone, a girl named Micki came by for him, but he never got up from the table when she arrived. My mother invited her to join us, but they disappeared into the night. I thought that would be the last time I would see him.

In January of 1971, I was in L.A. trying to sell my songs. I went back to Don Altfeld's office at 8961 Sunset Boulevard (Don was the co-writer of "The Little Old Lady From Pasadena"), where I had had luck two years earlier and suddenly found myself face to face with P.F. Sloan. I had seen him pop in and out of the Troubadour, where Jimmy Webb was singing his song about the reclusive Sloan. ("I have been seeking P.F. Sloan, but no one knows where he has gone...") He vaguely remembered his dinner in New York, but he was gracious and still a little strange. We sat on the floor, and I played him a song I wrote for the film *Love Story* entitled "Jenny." He was very much impressed and told Don and me that he wanted to record it. There was one small problem: I had promised it to an actor/singer by the name of Sam Chew earlier that week. I had a choice: an actor I had never heard of or my idol? There was no contest. I broke the news to Chew, who was not very happy to say the least. Unfortunately, it was not a good decision. Phil never recorded the song, and I didn't have Chew to go back to. "Jenny" never got recorded by anyone. (Chew went on to star in a 1980 film called *Serial*, as well as portraying both John and Bobby Kennedy on television.)

From 1971 until 1985, I still tried to stay in touch with Phil. He got stranger and stranger — sometimes he would deny it was he answering the phone. Other times he simply hung up on me — no explanation. Just a dial tone. For some masochistic reason or another, I never gave up. Then one day I spoke to Allan Pepper, who ran The Bottom Line nightclub here in New York City. I told him about Phil and how I thought it would

In James Dean's apartment, 6/3/85.

be a momentous occasion to have him perform there. He agreed. I called Phil and this time he was receptive, if not a little apprehensive.

I arranged the music and the musicians and had Phil stay with me and my then wife, Darla. Our first night together was spent in James Dean's original New York apartment. I had taken him to the address on West Sixty-Eighth Street on a lark. Little did we know we would run into the current occupant, who actually invited us in. Phil was fascinated. I also, by default, turned into the publicist as well, securing interviews for Phil with newspapers, radio, and television. The shows were a great success. People like Eric Andersen and Jimmy Webb showed up. I was very proud. Things had come full circle. Phil had made my developmental years more tolerable with his great music, and I was able to reciprocate with these comeback concerts. At the conclusion of his whirlwind New

York engagement, he bought me my first and only leather jacket. I still wear it, albeit worn and torn by New York City moths.

Phil continues to make periodic performances and recordings. He also continues to disappear.

The Bottom Line, June 1985.

Sloan, Andersen & Webb after the show.

Bobby Kennedy campaigning in New York City.

BOBBY KENNEDY

I don't know if this quite fits into the title of this book, but I really wanted to mention it. Sometime in the spring of 1968, I was coming home on the 104 Broadway bus from high school. While looking out the window, I could see a crowd forming on Seventy-Fifth Street and Broadway. Since I had a bus pass that allowed me to get on and off the bus wherever I wanted, I decided to investigate what the hubbub was all about.

There was a flatbed truck parked in front of a fish store called Citarella — still there today. I actually had never been in that store, since it was about a mile from my house, and I wasn't into fish — especially raw. (My love for sushi came much later.)

As I looked up, there was a man shaking people's hands and giving out free fish supplied by Citarella. Did it matter that this man was actually Bobby Kennedy? Well, sort of. I was also intrigued by the free fish deal.

So I pushed my way through the crowd to get to where Mr. Kennedy could see me and perhaps interact with me. We made eye contact, and he handed me a shrimp. I immediately popped it into my mouth and shook his hand.

Suddenly, the taste of the raw shrimp overtook me and I couldn't believe how disgusting it was. I had to spit it out, but I didn't want the Senator to see that, so I waited until he turned his head as I slipped away back into the crowd. Fortunately, I found a place in the gutter for my refuse of mashed shrimp.

I jumped back on the Broadway bus and headed home. I didn't grasp the importance of this encounter until years later, when I put the time frame together and realized Bobby Kennedy was assassinated in June of that same year.

JAY & THE AMERICANS AND...

Okay, this isn't about Jay & the Americans as much as it is about someone else. Let me explain…

In 1968, when I was sixteen years old, I was brought up to the Brill Building by songwriters Pete Andreoli and Vince Poncia. They had had hits as the Videls ("Mr. Lonely"), The Tradewinds ("New York's a Lonely Town") and The Innocence ("There's Got To Be a Word!"). They also had their songs recorded by everyone from Elvis to the Ronettes. I idolized them and even ended up with a song published by them that same year when they started their own production, publishing, and record company, Map City, a few blocks away on Fifty-Fifth Street. They were also producing a one-shot single for their friends Jay & the Americans.

This Brill Building office was called JATA Productions — and I am sure you can figure out what that stands for. I recall guys like Marty Sanders and the others just hanging around, sitting on the sides of their desks in their sparse surroundings. But there was something else going on in that office. It was the lone sound of an ancient upright piano. Playing that piano was an ancient man — a man you didn't expect to be there with all these rock and roll twenty-somethings. I had no idea who he was or why he was even there. It just didn't fit. Curiosity got the better of me so I asked one of the guys.

"Who's that old man over there?"

"Oh, that's this old time songwriter, Harry Woods," one of the Americans replied. "He shares this space with us when he's in town."

I didn't think much about it until years later. I had been in the room with a songwriting legend. This man literally wrote the songs the whole world sang. Songs like "When the Red, Red Robin (Keeps Bob-Bob Bobbin' Along)," "I'm Looking Over a Four Leaf Clover," and a great song I knew from a Hayley Mills rendition, "Side By Side." He wrote several of these songs by himself. My grandfather introduced many of his standards, including "Try a Little Tenderness."

At the time that I encountered him, he was already seventy-two years old. He had less than two years to live. But here he was working in the environment he was used to. Pounding away at the keyboard. And when I say pounding, I mean pounding. You see, Woods was born with no fingers on his left hand, so he compensated by playing hard with his stump, building up some big time calluses on that hand in order to play the bass parts on his songs with panache.

Left: *Map City at 236 West 55th St., now razed.* Right: *Harry Woods.*

Legend has it this man also had quite a temper. I will tell you a story within my story that had me so enthralled when I first heard it…

It seems there was a little bar downstairs in a place near the corner of Forty-Ninth Street and Broadway. It's still there (#220), but now it's called Da Marino (and by the time you read this, it will probably be called something else!) Back then, it was appropriately called Tin Pan Alley. It was a hangout for the ASCAP songwriters who liked to have a drink or two (or in this case, several) after work — or during work? Anyway, Woods would frequent the joint and was known to get quite volatile after knocking back a few. One night, Woods got into an altercation with another patron and had him on the floor, literally beating the daylights out of him. Unfortunately for the man, he was pummeling him with that callused left hand of his. Upon seeing this frightening scene, one patron called ASCAP and said, "You better get over here, that guy who wrote 'Try a Little Tenderness' is beating the crap out of someone!"

MYSTERY MAN

It was the summer of '69, and I was visiting California for the first time on my own to rekindle my flickering flame of a relationship with my childhood crush, Cindy. Unfortunately, that flame burned out about the first week on arrival, but I was there for more: to sell some songs of mine to West Coast publishers. I was sporting only a moustache at this time — the beard came at nineteen. I had gotten permission to grow it from my high school principal — yes, I actually asked her if I could grow it in the last months before graduation. She was not very happy with me, as I had declined to take those horrible SATs because I knew I wasn't going to attend college. I absolutely wanted to follow my dream of becoming an established songwriter, and this trip to L.A. was going to be happening as soon as I got out of that prison called school. However, it seemed no one would ever dream of skipping college in those years — but I did.

I managed to get a $500 advance from ASCAP — the musical organization that pays songwriters their royalties for airplay, and I paid it back the same year. Armed with my Guild Mark IV guitar — which I still own — and my portfolio of songs, I made my way to L.A. to stay with childhood friend Steve Beaver and his family. Staying with Steve proved to be a little strange inasmuch as his mother had a lights-out-at-eleven policy. This seemed slightly ridiculous, since I was now seventeen and technically on my own. But for free room and board, I couldn't quibble.

One day, I remember coming back a little later than usual from a hard time selling songs and arriving at the Beaver house at around 7 p.m. Keep in mind, I had no driver's license, so I had to get around by hitching and walking from Hollywood all the way to the Los Angeles neighborhood where I was staying. This was miles and miles. Mrs. Beaver told me there was no dinner left because I had not been there on time. I shrugged and made my way down a block or two to Pico Boulevard where there was an Orange Julius. I had the drink and a hot dog and called it a night.

The next day, I set out to sell some songs once again. It was now August, and hitchhikers like myself were not getting rides as easily; Charles Manson and family had just slaughtered Sharon Tate and many others, and the mood in Los Angeles toward hairy guys with a thumb out was very wary. Still, I tried my best, guitar in hand, and managed to get the attention of a goatee-sporting man who drove up to me standing on the corner of Beverly Drive and Little Santa Monica. He asked where I was going, and I told him a block past Pico on Edris Drive in Los Angeles. He told me he could take me up to Pico. I hopped in, and

Above: *In front of the Beaver house.* Below: *My aunt and uncle's house.*

he asked me about my music, and I asked him what he did. He said he was also a musician. The ride was short, so we didn't exchange very much information. I thanked him for the lift and made my way up the block to the Beavers' house.

My uncle Robert and aunt Natalie lived next door, and I suppose it looked kind of bad that I was staying with their neighbor and not them,

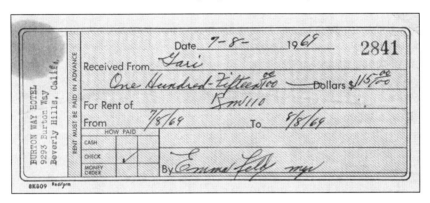

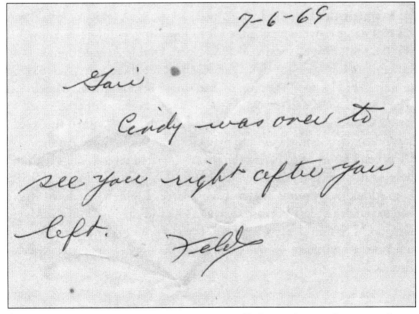

Above: *A month's rent at The Burton Way.* Below: *A typical message from Emma.*

so they offered to take me in. I was pleased, until Robert said upon my entrance, "You can stay one week and then your bags will be on the doorstep." Damn, a week? I needed to stay in L.A. longer than that.

I moved into the Burton Way Hotel at 9293 Burton Way — later torn down for a fancier hotel — which was a little like the Bates Motel in *Psycho*. It was run by a portly old lady named Emma Feld, who had an annoying dog named Jo Jo. You could hear her calling that dog at various times of the day and night. I had a depressing little room and bath, and there was a community refrigerator — all for $35 a week. There were times when I was desperate and actually looked inside the fridge only to find rancid butter in an old white plastic holder. There were no cell phones back then, and you had to rely on Emma to take messages for you when you were out. Not a very dependable service if you were a struggling songwriter waiting for that special call, or if you were a young available gent hoping to get an invitation from someone who might want to paint the town with you.

I eventually got an apartment in Hollywood at the Imperial Orchid Apartment House with another friend from New York, Larry Chernoff, and a songwriter I met in L.A. named Don Rogers. (Roger Donald was his real name — why he changed it to Don Rogers I'll never know!) It was built in 1959 and located at 1767 North Orchid Avenue right behind Grauman's Chinese Theater. Our rent to split three ways was $175 a month WITH a pool! We even took in singer-actress Andrea Marcovicci, who needed a place to stay while she went out on auditions. She used to have a stuffed animal, which she clung to all the time. When she would leave the apartment, we used to play kickball with it. Sorry Andrea.

When I returned to NY in the fall, having sold several songs with the help of the late Gary Zekley, "Little Old Lady From Pasadena" writer Don Altfeld, and professional manager Harvey Lippert, I sat down on my bed to watch a little TV. I came across a folk trio singing "Puff the Magic Dragon." I couldn't believe my eyes. The guy who gave me a ride — the unidentified musician — was none other than Paul Stookey from Peter, Paul & Mary!

The Imperial Orchid Apartments.

Left to Right: *Brian, Don, Larry.*

Jan's Corvette after the crash, April 12, 1966.

JAN & DEAN

Unfortunately, I can't say I had a close relationship with Jan. Jan Berry, the producer, writer, and lead singer of the duo Jan & Dean, was extremely handsome, extremely talented, and extremely self-destructive. After having a huge amount of surfing and hot rod hits with partner Dean Torrence, he was at the top of his game in April, 1966. They had TV pilots, movies, a proposed record label of their own, and many songs ready to be released. At age twenty-five he had a lot to live for. But, despite completing two years of medical school, the draft board was breathing down his neck. It was the time of the Vietnam War — not exactly the time you want to be drafted or have your successful career sabotaged.

On April 12, 1966, Jan crashed his Corvette into a parked truck belonging to a gardener, near UCLA in Los Angeles. He sustained horrendous injuries, which included brain damage — creating partial paralysis of his right side. It was thought he wouldn't survive, let alone ever sing and perform again. He loved Laurel and Hardy, so his manager, Lou Adler, rented a projector, along with the comedy team's films, to try to get Jan to come out of his long coma. He eventually did. The recovery was very difficult for him.

Meanwhile, Dean tried to keep their image alive, releasing an album privately on his own J&D label. The front cover pictured Dean and a very close facsimile to Jan — his brother Ken. All of this was the design of Dean himself — a very gifted graphic artist. It was during this period that I got to know this very warm gentleman with a great, dry sense of humor.

When I came out to California in 1969 at age seventeen, one of my aims was to meet Dean. I also met up with songwriter/producer Gary Zekley, writer of the Jan & Dean release "Yellow Balloon," which was featured on the Dean-produced album. The new publisher of my song "Bright Spectrum of Colors," was Don Altfeld, who happened to be a longtime friend and songwriting collaborator of Jan & Dean's as well as a close friend of Gary's. You can see how all of these people were connected.

I looked up Dean and called him to see if we could meet. He said he would be delighted, and I made my way down Sunset Boulevard to 7777 (also 7783-7785), near Genesee Avenue, in Hollywood. Dean had a little office complex in a wonderful building from 1895. (Coincidentally, that location would later be the home of Hollywood Sheet Music, where they sold my song folios.)

Home of Kitty Hawk Graphics.

Dean: "Developers wanted to knock down the old building and build a mini-mall. The city designated the building as a historical structure and it had to stay as is. Although it hardly ever rains in Southern California, one night, Jewish lightning hit the old building and burned it down. Lo and behold, up popped a mini-mall. Imagine that!"

I climbed the stairs and found myself in a crowded space called Kitty Hawk Graphics. Dean had already done some gorgeous and creative album covers for the likes of the Turtles and Bobby Vee. He later won a Grammy in 1972 for his fascinating cover for an album called Pollution, which featured a tiny chick breaking from his egg with a gas mask on his face.

We had a great time exchanging shop talk about his days as Jan & Dean — how he was surviving the demise of the duo and how Jan was. I had already encountered some gossip about Jan when I was up at Don

Altfeld's office, when a guy came by looking exactly like Jan. I asked Don if it was indeed Jan, and he said it wasn't.

"Remember 'Jeanette Get your Hair Done' [an old Jan & Dean tune]?" Don asked me.

"Yes, of course," I replied.

"Well, that was the result," Don answered.

The implication was this was an out of wedlock child from that union of Jan and Jeanette. Indeed, Steve Berry was the son I mistook for Jan that day. (Update: Jeannette passed away on October 29, 2010, at the age of sixty-eight from lung cancer. Their son Steve died of AIDS on November 18, 1995.)

While Dean and I were speaking, he showed me the album he had pressed up as Jan & Dean. It was called "Save For a Rainy Day." He gave it to me. I was so thrilled. You can't imagine how excited I

The album Dean gave me.

was to get a copy of this original album that was a true collector's item. Not many were pressed. I thanked him and promised to stay in touch.

I would write to Dean and tell him my career updates, and he always wrote back — in handwritten notes. His large writing reflected the artistic designing he was known for at this point. He was in big demand.

In 1972, I sent him a song I had out at the time called "Bicycle Ride." He loved it. He said he even played it for Mike Love of the Beach Boys, and he loved it, too. Dean kept this song in mind until he had a chance to produce it with an artist. And true to his word, that's just what he did.

He found a group called Locksley Hall. They sounded a lot like Chicago, a very popular group and sound at that time (circa 1974). He decided it was right for them. And they did record it. I recall getting this news in another handwritten letter from Dean, when I opened my mail on the way to the beach (ironically) on a New York City subway. Unfortunately, they didn't get a deal right away and broke up before my song could be released.

In 1978, Dean put me in touch with his new manager, Winston Simone. Jan & Dean had been enjoying a revival of sorts. A movie had been done on their lives, and there was a demand to see them again. Jan's

July 18, 1974

Dear Brian,

Believe it or not, I just got around to listening to your tape. I love Bicycle Ride, and would love to record it. I played it for Bruce and Terry and they liked it as well. Now the only problem is that we have more material than we know what to do with. I have a feeling that the criteria used for picking the tunes we will record will probably have alot to do with publishing, so my question to you is, would it be possible to split some publishing so as to give "Bicycle Ride" an advantage over the other favorites that are un-splitable publishing wise. Bruce and Terry are very concious of publishing and are very much in- fluanced by it in relation to what tunes they will or will not record. Anyway, do what you can and let me know as quickly as possible.

Thanks.........

Dean

DEAN O. TORRENCE
7785 SUNSET BLVD. HOLLYWOOD, CALIF. 90046
PHONE 876-1534

speech was still kind of slurred, and his leg dragged as a result of that crash twelve years earlier. But he was making a real effort to have a comeback. They had a great band behind them called Papa Doo Run Run, and they had nostalgia on their side.

I was made aware of all the places they would be while in New York. I attended most everything, and Dean was glad to see me again. He told me

A group shot from The Palladium. I'm at the top looking to my left. Dean is at the bottom right with two drinks while Jan is at the bottom left.

they were scheduled to play the Palladium on East Fourteenth Street — sadly, now gone — and he asked me if I'd like to perform on stage with them. I was delighted, to say the least! I knew all the songs anyway.

So there I was, on July 15, 1978, singing my heart out on "Barbara Ann" — a song not only recorded by Jan & Dean but a record that Dean sang on when the Beach Boys covered it. Things had come full circle for me.

As we left the theater, Dean and I were walking down the street when he spied a street pole that had been bent in two. He simply remarked, "Oh,

With Dean in Huntington Beach, CA, 2002.

Jan must have been here." Bad taste? That was Dean's sense of humor. I found it hysterical.

What wasn't funny was the passing of Jan in 2004. He had recovered as much as he could, but that accident took its toll on him, and he died at the age of sixty-two.

Dean and I have stayed in touch through the years. In fact, in 2002, I interviewed him for the *E True Hollywood Story* of the Beach Boys. It was fun to reunite with him for that project and to hang out with him at his Huntington Beach home. He is a true Californian with his blonde hair, golden tan, and home just steps away from the beach. We had our picture taken together, which graced my CD "Brian Sings Wilson." His music is youthful and that's probably what keeps this man in his seventies looking so young!

CAROLE KING PART 1

On January 5, 1971, the day after I arrived in L.A., I had an appointment at A&M Records. A&M was located at 1416 North LaBrea in Hollywood. This was formally Charlie Chaplin's studios, followed by Red Skelton's offices, as well a CBS television facility. Chaplin built the English-style cottage-type offices and sound stages in 1917. He even had his footprints in the cement. Herb Alpert and Jerry Moss bought the entire place from CBS for $1 million in 1966. It is now owned by the Jim Henson Company.

My appointment was with the well-known sax player Curtis Amy. He was a musician in high demand, but held a position at A&M where he would see new songwriters and artists like myself. He was extremely kind, and we chatted about my influences. One such major influence was Carole King. I had written her a fan letter in 1966, when she was still married to her writing partner, Gerry Goffin, and they lived in New

The A&M Records complex.

Jersey. I never received an answer. In 1967, when I met Neil Sedaka at his publishers, Screen Gems, I mentioned her name to him. I asked if she was attractive: he made a face. He told me she wore wigs, and she wasn't his type at all — interesting, given the rumor he started that "Oh Carol" was written about her when they were "dating." Carole has been pissed at him ever since.

The Carole King recording session with Ralph Schuckett on far right.

Somewhere in the conversation, Curtis asked me if I'd like to meet Carole. I was thrilled by the invitation. He said to come back in two days at four o'clock, and he would arrange a meeting. He had been playing sax on her newest album, and she was right next door in the recording studio.

I arrived exactly on time and met with Curtis. He brought me up to the studio and had me sit in the control room, while I watched keyboardist, Ralph Schuckett, work out an overdub on a song I had never heard before. It seemed really catchy. When he was done, Carole and I stepped into a little area all by ourselves. She wrapped herself up in a chair while I sat across from her. She was much more attractive than Sedaka had indicated. She was very small and very cute in her tight blue jeans. Her eyes were a gorgeous sky blue, and she was very friendly.

She asked about me, and I told her how much she influenced my writing and how I had written to her in New Jersey some years back. We chatted about her past songs, her 1968 album as part of the group The City, as well as her 1970 release "Writer" — she was very much impressed with my knowledge of her catalog. She then asked me if I could recommend any songs she had forgotten about that she might be able to record herself. I came up with a couple. She was so sweet to me, but I realized my time was up and she had to get back to recording.

By the way, the song Schuckett was overdubbing his keyboard on was "Where You Lead." The album? *Tapestry*.

WEST BANK CAFE
DOWNSTAIRS THEATRE BAR

PRESENTS

A MINOR INCIDENT

a one act play

Written by: HINDI BROOKS
Directed by: AARON SPEISER

starring

Carole King

with

Paul Hipp
Jack Hannibal
Richard Kidney

NOVEMBER
8:30 .... 11·12·13
8:30 & 10:30 14
10:30 .... 18· 19·
20· 21

RESERVATIONS: 212 □ 695 □ 6909
407 WEST 42ND ST

CAROLE KING PART 2

In 1988, I discovered Carole was going to make her stage debut in an off-Broadway show entitled *A Minor Incident*, on Forty-Second Street at the West Bank Cafe. This was a straight part and had nothing to do with her musical side.

I got a ticket for myself and sat down in the middle of the smallish room. The lights went down, and the audience experienced a car crash, if I recall correctly. Carole came out into the audience and started screaming, "Will you help me? Will you help me?"

She was right in my face asking this question, and I was on the spot. I truly had no idea if she wanted me actually to participate in the play or not. I was very embarrassed and was at a total loss as to what to do. If I answered her, would I screw up the play? If I didn't respond, was I being an idiot when King was acting so desperately? I decided to remain quiet and lay low.

After the show, I went backstage. I tried to have a conversation with her, but it didn't go so well. She was very much distracted, and I simply left.

Jump to 2012, when Carole was going to be at Barnes & Noble signing copies of her new autobiography. I wanted the book and thought it might possibly be fun to remind her of our first meeting. I stood in a long line, and I knew I only had seconds to speak to her when I reached the table.

"Hi Carole…you won't believe this, but we are probably the only two people here that were at the 'Tapestry' sessions."

She smiled and said, "No…my daughter over there (Sherry) was also at the studio. Nice to see you again."

It wasn't much of a reunion. Once more, she was distracted, but I did get my book signed.

JOHNNY GREEN AND *FRIENDS*

In the beginning of 1971, I was in Los Angeles to try to sell my songs once again. I moved into the Park Sunset at 8462 Sunset Boulevard. (It's now the upscale Grafton and the Olive Kitchen & Bar.) I was paying about $155 a month. It turned out to be a hangout for comedians like Nipsey Russell — who caused a ruckus there one night over a girl — and Gene Baylos — more on him later.

I would sit in the lobby kibitzing with them, when all of a sudden they would see a car, jump up and shout "there's Joey!" Meaning Joey Bishop. He was one of the few people on TV still hiring the old timers, like their friend Leonard Barr (Dean Martin's uncle).

I had just seen the songwriter Jimmy Webb ("MacArthur Park," "By the Time I Get To Phoenix," and "Wichita Lineman") in New York the previous December, and I was surprised to see him playing in L.A. at the legendary Troubadour. I had just met him and the band at the Bitter End in Greenwich Village and was pleased that he was making an appearance again. I met up with his band, who were equally pleased to see me, and who sneaked me in every night through the back door. (Thank you, Skip Mosher.)

The opening act was the brilliant Judee Sill, who I had never heard of before. I was mesmerized. Her songs were so intriguing and melodic. She was also odd. When she went to the piano from the guitar to play "Enchanted Sky Machines," she let out a burp that reverberated throughout the entire club. Most people couldn't believe it. But Judee was a toughie with a heart of gold. Although the stepdaughter of a Tom and Jerry animator, she was thrown into reform schools and ended up on the street with a heroin addiction, prostituting herself. Somehow, her music began to win out, and she had her song "Lady-O" recorded by the Turtles, which became a hit. David Geffen signed her, and she made two gorgeous albums for him. I was drawn to a song called "The Archetypal Man,"

The signed harpsichord part from Judee.

which had a harpsichord part in the beginning that Judee would duplicate with her voice at every show. And I would request the song every night. At the end of the run, she actually gave me the printed harpsichord part, which I cherish to this day. Unfortunately, she succumbed to her addiction in 1979, at age thirty-five. A great loss as a talent and human being.

When Webb performed, I yelled obscure song titles, like the exquisite "Evie," to which he would look at me and then the band and say, "Let's leave her out of it!" During these repeated visits to the Troubadour, I made friends with a very sweet girl named Sandi, who drove us to and from the club every night in her old broken down Ford Falcon she affectionately called Freida.

At the last show, I was sitting next to a girl who was amazed at all I knew about Jimmy Webb. We got to talking, and she told me she knew him and that she was a songwriter too. We hit it off and exchanged numbers. Her name was Kathe Green, seven and a half years my senior. She had indeed recorded a whole album in England for the Deram label just two years earlier, when she was dating Richard Harris. A day or two later, she came to pick me up at my aunt and uncle's new place in Beverly Hills — I was staying there until I got the room at the Park Sunset.

Kathe had some small Band-Aids on her face from some recent surgery that she said was the result of some sun damage. She whisked me away in her sports car to her father's house at 903 North Bedford Drive, where she was staying. We plopped down in his work room where we

Left: *Sandi sent me this Xerox in the early '70s — real 8x10s cost too much!* Right: *Johnny Green.*

With Kathe at my uncle Robert's piano.

exchanged songs. I loved hers — she loved mine. We learned each other's songs right then and there, and we formed a little act. Appropriately, we actually performed that little act on February 15, at The Ye Little Club in the heart of Beverly Hills.

But in that work room, we traded story after story, discussing our likes and dislikes, which included my aversion to meats like tongue. Sometime

Jean Negulesco

during our discussion, her father walked in. I had no idea who he was, but I soon found out. It was Johnny Green, the composer of standards like "Body and Soul" and "I Cover the Waterfront." He scored films like *Raintree County* and conducted for the Oscars. He even wrote the Betty Boop theme song! There he was with his carnation in his lapel, asking Kathe if her "new friend" would like to stay for dinner. Well, considering I had no idea where my next meal was coming from, I enthusiastically accepted.

We moved into the dining room, and I sat down at the table. They asked what I would like to drink, and I simply said "a Coke would be fine." They had a servant bring out the dinner. I couldn't believe my eyes. It was a big, flapping tongue! Yes, my most hated food. And it had a raisin sauce on it. There were also mashed potatoes. Little did I know that in addition to Mr. Green being an award winning composer and conductor, he was also a gourmet cook who traded recipes with none other than Dinah Shore! Well, what could I do? I had to eat this meal. I started to gag on the tongue. (A comedian once said that he doesn't like anything that can taste you back!) I started to take the mashed potatoes and try to disguise the tongue inside them. Mr. Green noticed this and raised his voice slightly to say, "If you don't like it, just say so, and the maid will make you a hamburger!" I sheepishly responded affirmatively and hoped my time at the table would end soon.

Kathe would drive me around the winding curves of Mulholland to meet her friends — and what an amazing bunch they were. We landed at Jack Palance's home — he and I shared the same birthday. The expansive digs overlooked L.A. We spent a little time with his daughters Holly and

Brooke, who were both close to my age. We also hung out with Patsy Sullivan (daughter of actor Barry and later to marry — and divorce — Jimmy Webb.) Her friend Warren Seabury came along as well. Patsy was crying over Jimmy Webb's latest disappearance from her life. (She was only fifteen at this time. They eventually married in 1974.) We all went out to see *Brewster McCloud* in Westwood that Friday night.

Kathe and I continued performing our songs, and Johnny Green thought we were pretty good. We sang a few songs in the living room one night with Louis Jourdan and the great film director and Green neighbor, Jean Negulesco, in attendance. I had no idea who Negulesco was, but he was very nice. Turns out he directed *Johnny Belinda*, *Phone Call From a Stranger*, *Three Coins In the Fountain* (with Jourdan), *How To Marry a Millionaire*, and countless others!

The next day, while I was trying to sell my songs, I got back to the hotel a little later than usual, and there was a message in my box from Kathe. I guess we made an impression on the Green family because it seems that Dinah Shore had wanted us to come for dinner that night and perform for her. Too late. I missed my chance and the opportunity never arose again.

JOHNNY MATHIS

Before it was home of the DuMont Television System in 1954 and named WABD, 205 East Sixty-Seventh Street between Third and Second Avenues was originally the Jacob Ruppert Central Opera House. Many early stars of television worked there. By 1958, it changed its call letters to WNEW and its name to Metropolitan Broadcasting Corporation. In the same year, David Susskind did his *Open End* show from there. In fact, when a young singer by the name of Barbra Streisand lived around the corner on Third Avenue in an old walk-up tenement, she would often drop in on Susskind's talk show.

I grew up watching the station when shows like Sonny Fox's *Wonderama* and stars like Sandy Becker and Soupy Sales broadcast from there. It was now called Metromedia Television, and in 1965, when Soupy was suspended by the station for an innocent prank, the kids all gathered outside and picketed the station.

There was also a local television show there in the late '60s called *The New Yorkers*, hosted by Skitch Henderson. It was a combination talk/music show that aired over WNEW Channel 5. It eventually evolved into a show called *Midday Live* in the '70s when the host was Bill Boggs.

The late Joe Pellegrino was the professional manager for one of my earliest publishers. In fact, like it or not, he was the man who encouraged me to sing my own songs. I will always be grateful to him. His time on earth was cut short when he lost his sight and his life due to AIDS. He was also very intelligent and knew how to get songs recorded — though sadly, not one of mine.

He once told me in 1968 — while he was at the Croma Music publishers where he was publishing my songs — that he got a song to Robert Goulet while waiting outside the Copa where Goulet was performing. I was impressed with his tenacity, and it inspired me to do the same for years and years. (Not that it ever worked, but it was better than sitting at home!)

So, I took his concept to heart and made good use of it when I heard Johnny Mathis was going to be on *Midday* in the mid-1970s. I packed my bag with an acetate of a song I deemed perfect for Mathis — "The

Non-Affair Affair" (later recorded by the actress Jana Robbins.) It was pressed up on an acetate, as most songwriters' demos were in those days. This was long before CDs, mp3s, and the lot. We weren't even sending out cassettes yet. It was a disc that cost three bucks every time we had to have one pressed up. Yes, there was more of an investment for songwriters in those days. You actually used a real recording studio to cut your demos and then pressed up samples to give away, in the hopes someone would put the needle on the disc and shout "Hooray…I just heard my next number one record!"

I got on my bike and made the pilgrimage across town to the Channel 5 studios. As I said, the show was called *Midday Live*, so I knew Mathis was actually going to be there in the late morning. There was also no security back then, so there was no paranoia about a struggling songwriter walking through the doors of the studio to approach someone like Mathis.

I went directly into the Green Room, where I found Mathis sitting there. I introduced myself.

"Hi Johnny, my name is Brian Gari and I'm a songwriter and have admired you for years. I just wrote this song, which I hope you'll consider."

His response was great.

"Hi Brian. Nice to meet you. Of course I'll listen. Thanks for thinking of me."

I couldn't have been happier with his response. No one there to stop me. No one there to interfere. Just me and Mathis. I was thrilled — well almost. Something was nagging at me as I was leaving. It had almost been too easy. A thought kept running through my head. Is he actually going to take the disc in the envelope with him when he leaves? He would have to do his performance and then remember that hit song I gave him as he exited the studio. I devised a plan.

I left Channel 5, walked across Sixty-Seventh Street, and hid behind a car. Yep, I actually decided to wait there until Mathis walked out the only door onto the street. It wasn't long before I saw him leave. I noticed he did not have the envelope under his arm. I casually crossed the street where he could see me. He immediately looked at me, smiled, and gestured he had forgotten my disc and went right back into the studio to retrieve it.

I lounged around the street until Johnny came back out, and there he was, Brian's envelope in hand, as he continued his walk up to Third Avenue. I was very proud of myself. It was a confrontation of sorts, but nothing mean. Of course, he never did record the song.

GLEN CAMPBELL

It had always been my dream to have one of my songs recorded by Glen Campbell. None ever were. And believe me, it wasn't for my lack of trying. I searched everywhere for direct addresses: his home, his office, I even stood backstage at a concert. Nothing ever worked. I really felt I had so many songs that were right for him, but alas, it just didn't happen. (And sadly, with Glen's recent diagnosis of Alzheimer's, it will never happen.)

One day when I was about twenty-three, my publisher, who was also a writer, made me an offer I couldn't refuse. He said if I could get his one particular song recorded by a name artist, he would give me a cut of the royalties. I figured I had nothing to lose and everything to gain — except possibly a reputation for plugging other people's songs instead of my own.

The first suggestion was Barry Manilow. I don't think I got a response from him. The rejections didn't matter. I didn't love the song and it wasn't mine, so I never took it personally.

One day, the name Glen Campbell came up. I really didn't want to appear to Glen — if he was actually paying attention — that I was just a lackey who was out there plugging everyone's songs. So I designed a plan. I had heard about people creating pseudonyms for other business ventures, so why not me? That way, if Glen and I ever worked together in the future, it would be based solely on my work, and there wouldn't be any mention of my history of pushing other people's tunes.

Thus I became Roger Newman. The name sounded nice and generic. I made a copy of my publisher's song and typed up a polite letter on "Roger Newman" stationery. I found Glen's office address, which seemed to be accurate, and sent off a package that included these words:

Dear Mr. Campbell:
I hope you can find time to listen to this great song that was just given to me by one of our writers here. I think it could be your next hit.

Sincerely,
Roger Newman

I took it to the post office and pretty much forgot about it. I had my own songs to plug.

A few weeks later, on November 5, 1975, there was a letter waiting for me with the return address of Glen Campbell. I quickly ripped it open and read this:

Dear Mr. Newman:

Thank you for submitting your original material to me for my consideration. Needless to say, I appreciate your interest in me and my music company.

I wish I could give you a favorable response; however, I don't think your material is right for me at this time.

Don't give up!! Here's wishing you success in the future.

Sincerely Yours,
Glen

It was actually signed by Glen! I couldn't believe it — the one time I submitted another person's song, Glen answers me personally! I had his ear for that one moment and he was listening to someone else's goddamn song!

Thank you, Roger Newman.

Glen Campbell

November 5, 1975

Dear Mr. Newman:

Thank you for submitting your original material to me for my consideration. Needless to say, I appreciate your interest in me and my music company.

I wish I could give you a favorable response; however, I don't think that your material is right for me at this time.

Don't give up!! Here's wishing you success in the future.

Sincerely yours,

Glen Campbell

GC/uk

RODNEY DANGERFIELD

I loved Rodney. I grew up watching him on various variety shows in the '60s, such as *Ed Sullivan*. His everyman routine of "I don't get no respect" was hysterical — and clean. In fact, when I was performing at Pips in Sheepshead Bay, the owner, George Schultz — known as "the ear" for his ability to know good comedy and talented comedians — gave

Left: *George Schultz in his comic days as Georgie Starr.* Right: *George when I knew him in the late '70s.* Above: *George's club Pips in Sheepshead Bay.*

Rodney the "no respect" routine. George had been a comic decades earlier under the name Georgie Starr, but had retired his material in favor of starting his own venue.

Rodney was born Jacob Cohen, but changed his name professionally to Jack Roy after his show biz uncle, Roy Arthur. Ironically, Roy Arthur was partners with Jean Bedini in vaudeville — employing a very young Eddie Cantor. Arthur was affectionately known by his nickname, Bunky, in the Cantor household. In fact, when I mentioned my grandfather to Rodney years later at a comedy club, Rodney also referred to his uncle as Bunky.

John DeBellis

As Jack Roy, Rodney played the Catskills in the '40s and '50s, but had just mediocre success, resulting in his giving up the business to earn a real living by selling aluminum siding on Long Island. However, show biz was deep in his blood, and he eventually tried it again in the mid-1960s. It was at this point that Rodney took on his new professional name of Rodney Dangerfield and began utilizing Schultz's old bit of "no respect." He became a huge hit. He even ended up opening a nightclub on First Avenue called (what else?) Dangerfield's. (I've played there myself.) In fact, when you looked up the name Jack Roy in the Manhattan directory at that time, the phone number was Rodney's private office at that First Avenue address.

Rodney and I would run into each other a lot in the '70s. I was a regular at all three comedy clubs: the Comic Strip, the Improv, and Catch a Rising Star, performing my songs in between up-and-coming comics. One night in 1976, Rodney walked into the Comic Strip. He made it a regular custom to try out his seven minute bit for *Carson* at all three clubs, refining it and perfecting it for television. He also would throw in a few "blue" lines for the fun of it.

Comedian John DeBellis, a friend of mine and a writer-friend of Rodney's (comics would make $50 or $75 coming up with one liners for Rodney), yelled out to the stage, "Hey Rodney, what did you do for the Bicentennial?" Rodney would snap back, "I balled 200 chicks." And with that, Rodney would leave the stage to thundering laughter and applause. Well, I was among the laughing patrons, and I realized what a great bit it was. Now, if you think it stops there, think again…

As I said, Rodney liked to refine his routine, so what better way than to do it again at the next club. DeBellis would usually stay behind because he himself had a spot at the club an hour or so later. But Brian Gari had

Rodney at the Improv.

his own routine. I would book myself in all three clubs to make the $5 and take home the complimentary meals (cheeseburger or chef salad.) So when I went over a few blocks from the Comic Strip to Catch a Rising Star for my spot, who would also be there? Rodney! Rodney would go on immediately, bumping whoever else might be scheduled. We didn't mind. He was funny and a nice guy. So Rodney got up on the stage, and I watched from the wings.

When I saw he was reaching the end of his bit, I yelled out "Hey, Rodney — what did you do for the Bicentennial?" He answered like clockwork, "I balled 200 chicks." Again, a huge response, and Rodney was out the door to catch a cab to the Improv on West Forty-Fourth Street and Ninth Avenue.

Well, I had my moped, so I after my spot, I strapped my guitar to my back and zipped through the park to the West Side for my Improv spot.

And of course, there was Rodney at the bar about to go on! I sat in the back of the room again, and waited 'til the end of his routine and promptly asked, "Hey, Rodney — what did you do for the Bicentennial?" "I balled 200 chicks." The place went wild.

This didn't go on only during 1976, I did it every time I saw Rodney at the clubs — for years. Finally, after umpteen times of this bantering, I decided it was time to reveal myself. "Hey, Rodney — you know all those times you did the 'balling 200 chicks during the Bicentennial' bit?" I didn't have to say one more word. Rodney simply responded "Oh, that was you? Hey, thanks!"

Brian looking up at Ellie Greenwich during his Saturday Night Live
rehearsal, November 27, 1976.

BRIAN WILSON AND LORNE MICHAELS

A comedian by the name of Fred Raker was my roommate in 1976. We met at the Comic Strip comedy club and hit it off. He liked my music and I liked his comedy. To supplement his income, he took a job as a page at NBC. He knew how much I loved Brian Wilson, and when Brian was set to be a guest on the November 27 episode of *Saturday Night Live*, Fred arranged for me to have two passes to attend the rehearsals in the afternoon. (I wasn't at the actual show because I was performing myself that night.)

I decided to invite my friend Ellie Greenwich, since Brian's favorite song (and record) of all time was her "Be My Baby." When we arrived at the show — which was ironically taped in the same studio where my grandfather had done his radio show decades earlier — I let Brian's people know that I was there with Ellie. We were ushered up to the bleachers where we waited for Brian to come out.

Suddenly, there was my hero. He was still overweight and under the constant watch of the controversial Dr. Eugene Landy. (Dr. Landy later had to surrender his license for improper prescription of drugs and various improper personal and professional relationships, even acquiring parts of Wilson's copyrights. He died at age seventy-one in 2006.)

Brian sat down at the piano and looked up at the bleachers to see Ellie. He kept saying "Hi Ellie…Hi Ellie," waving his hand a little with each hello. It was sweet and strange at the same time. He was very childlike, but he was still my idol.

While he rehearsed "Back Home" and "Good Vibrations," I looked up at the monitors and saw something that disturbed me greatly. They were focusing not on Brian's face but on his leg, which was incessantly shaking underneath the piano. I gave the director a little time, but the camera seemed to be fixated on his leg. I did not find this funny. I found it exploitive. Producer Lorne Michaels was right there on the floor and well aware of this camera angle.

I couldn't take it anymore. I jumped out of the bleachers and practically flew down to where Michaels was standing. I straightforwardly asked if he was planning to use that kind of shot on the show that night. He asked me why. I immediately answered that I thought it was cruel to do that to a man who has given us so much joy. He looked at me for a moment — he could have had me thrown out — and said he would not use that shot. I

Brian Wilson & Ellie Greenwich backstage at BB King's in NYC, August 19, 2002.

watched the show from the upstairs room of the club I was playing that night — Pips in Sheepshead Bay, Brooklyn — and Michaels was true to his word: there were no shaky leg shots.

My connection with Brian became more interesting as the years went on. In 1995, I produced a CD for a Sony subsidiary, Risky Business, called "Got You Covered! Songs of the Beach Boys," which featured cover versions of some of Brian's songs. Then, in 2002, I worked on my most ambitious project yet: an entire album of me singing Brian's most interesting compositions. I called it "Brian Sings Wilson." I was most proud that Brian himself allowed me to write the lyric to his instrumental "Summer Means New Love."

In February of the same year, I was asked to help produce the *E True Hollywood Story* on the Beach Boys, where I interviewed some of the most important key players in their careers. People like Hal Blaine, Van Dyke Parks, Tony Asher, David Marks, and Dean Torrence were among the great folks with whom I got to speak. I even supplied background music — with my partner Jeff Olmsted, who also co-produced and co-arranged my "Brian Sings Wilson" project.

In August 2002, I had a lot of fun winning a contest to perform with the Beach Boys — although not with Brian — at Westbury, Long Island. I did, however, get to see Brian that same month at BB King's, where I handed him a copy of "Brian Sings Wilson." He seemed shocked, but pleased. A very humble guy.

Brian Wilson holding my CD backstage at the same event.

ROBIN WILLIAMS AND THE IMPROV

The Improvisation did not start out as a comedy club. Located at 358 West Forty-Fourth Street, close to Ninth Avenue in the heart of New York's Hell's Kitchen, the establishment was started in 1963. It was the brainchild of Broadway actress Silver Saundors and her husband, Budd Friedman. They were both in their early thirties at the time.

Silver had been in the original Broadway productions of *Fiorello!* and *How to Succeed In Business Without Really Trying.* She and Budd felt there should be a place to go after a Broadway show, where the actors could unwind and maybe do a song or two. Of course, there were comedians like Richard Pryor who would pop by, but it was primarily a musical kind of place.  It was a rather large room with a basic brick wall and another section with a bar and some booths where you could sit, drink, and have a snack.

A main entrance led you into the bar area, where you would be escorted into the main room with little tables, a minimal stage, and one microphone. One other door existed: the fire exit door that led directly onto West Forty-Fourth Street from the main room. Remember this.

In 1970, I was all of eighteen years old and very friendly with a musical comedy actress named Ilene Schatz (I still am.) She later became a major soap star under the name Ilene Kristen. She and I both loved Kenny Rankin, and I knew all his songs and played the same guitar as he did. She suggested we do one of those songs at The Improv (as it was affectionately called). I thought *what the heck.* I had very little experience performing live in a club, but I made the voyage downtown with Ilene and got a spot on the show.

As I went up to the stage, I noticed a songwriter in the audience and noted in my brain that I should acknowledge him when I was up on the stage. He was not yet a major star, but I loved his work. At the end of our number, I blurted out: "I would be remiss if I didn't acknowledge a great songwriter in our midst. This man wrote great songs for Neil Sedaka, and I think we should have a big hand for — PETER ALLEN!!!" Well, he

jumped out of his chair and yelled, "But I'm going on NEXT!" I had ruined his introduction. When we were coming off stage, Budd took me aside and said in no uncertain terms NEVER to do that again. I was extremely embarrassed.

The Improv was the only game in town until December 1972, when Rick Newman decided to open the East Side equivalent. Christened "Catch a Rising Star," the club really took off with a huge array of comedians and the

Ilene at about the time of the Improv.

usual middle-of-the-road singers. But the distance between the two didn't set off any real alarms with the Friedmans. However, all was not happy in the Friedman household, and the monocled Budd and his wife Silver were divorced by 1975. Budd went off to the West Coast, where he started a very popular Improv in Hollywood. Silver won the New York club in the divorce settlement and ran it by herself.

By 1979, the Improv and Silver had heard about how well I was doing at the Comic Strip and Catch a Rising Star and allowed me to perform there. Hey, it was another five bucks and a meal! So I would usually book myself at the East Side clubs first and then hop on my blue Solex moped and putt-putt over to West Forty-Fourth Street, guitar over my back. It was inevitable that my old twelve-string guitar would be horribly out of tune by the time I got there, so I would make a mad dash to the bar area, tune up, and go on stage. At first, I didn't want to utilize the band because of my previous experiences with the piano players at the other clubs. Many of them thought they were great jazz players — and some were — but that did not fit my pop-styled songs. So after a while, I thought it would be better if I simply accompanied myself.

Eventually, after hearing the incredible musicianship of the great piano players at the Improv, I tried them. Paul Greenwood and John Lenehan were fantastic. I couldn't have asked for better musicians to play my music. Sadly, John died of AIDS in 1987 at the age of thirty-six. He was so talented and very kind. I also utilized the drumming talents of Howie Klein, who went on to become a big agent.

Left: *The only known shot of me performing at the Improv — I stole it off their wall when I knew I wasn't coming back.* Above: *John Lenehan.*

I recall sitting in the bar area one night in the '70s, chatting with a very nice guy. He was bright and waiting, like me, for his time to go on. I never thought about him again until one night when I was watching a series called *One of the Boys* (and later on, *Saturday Night Live*). It was the Church Lady himself: Dana Carvey.

I believe it was sometime in the summer of 1980 that a very famous comedian popped by…In fact, he stopped by on more than one occasion. Robin Williams was a really great guy, and he knew the true definition of the word improvisation. The audience would go insane when he suddenly came up on the stage. He could make comedy out of the simplest things that he saw around him. And that's where I came in — literally.

Robin saw me drive up on my moped and thought we could do something clever with me and my vehicle. I couldn't imagine what, but he directed me as to what he wanted.

He said "At a certain time, when I open up the door from the main room to the street, I want you to drive your moped directly into the room in front of the stage."

Now, let me tell you something. Silver could be very, very mean and nasty, especially after a few drinks. She actually asked me to stop performing one of my most popular songs at the club "Letter To Norma." It

A group shot from the Improv, circa 1980, with Howie Klein to my right and Paul Greenwood at far right. John Lenehan is second from left in the row above and Silver is on the upper right.

had a line in it that said "the drinking's over." Hmmm…a connection? Anyway, I certainly didn't want to incur the wrath of this woman, but when the toss up is disappointing Robin Williams or pissing off Silver, there was no contest.

Therefore, at the designated moment, the door to Forty-Fourth Street burst open, and I drove my smelly, exhaust-fumed moped directly into the club.

Robin exclaimed, "Another fine prize you'll win on *The Price Is Right.*" The audience went ballistic. So did Silver, but I think she knew the value of the audience response and that people would be going home telling all their friends about what a great time they had at the Improv.

Today, all that's left of this wonderful club is the brick wall and a small plaque acknowledging the previous existence of the legendary venue. It is now the Don Giovianni Pizza Restaurant — but for how long?

Robin Williams and Budd Friedman.

Silver Friedman

GEORGIE JESSEL

Jessel was a lifelong friend of Eddie Cantor's. They went all the way back to the Gus Edwards troupe called Kid Kabaret in 1912. Jessel was fourteen and my grandfather was twenty. Cantor was like an older brother to Jessel, who really looked up to him, admired him, and truly loved him. When my grandfather had a second heart attack in 1957, on a nationally televised special, Jessel was right there to support him, showing great concern for his survival. He was also an embarrassment to my grandfather. His politics were skewed, his hair pieces were ridiculous, and his speeches were off center and corny; he lived for memorials where he could go on and on about the deceased. In fact, there's an old joke that went around that when Jessel was speaking at a funeral one time, he looked down at the coffin and exclaimed, "Oh my God — I knew that man!"

Cantor & Jessel in Kid Kabaret, circa 1912.

Eddie Cantor made it clear that when he died, he did not want a big funeral, and he left specific instructions NOT to let Jessel speak. That must have really cramped Jessel's style!

I knew Georgie when I was a child. He was always at my grandparents' house. Of course, I didn't know a whole lot about him other than he was in show business and was my grandfather's close friend.

By 1979, I started going with a woman who taught the deaf. Her aim was to teach theater to the deaf, and finally got a job doing just that. Unfortunately, it was in Washington, D.C. It was the first year of our relationship, and it certainly made things difficult. We came to the understanding that we would try to commute between New York and

D.C., which turned out to be mostly my responsibility. As I was making my living performing at the comedy clubs, I had to scramble to get booked in Washington. This was not an easy task, as no one knew — or cared — about booking me.

I started out at a club called Dot's Spot, which turned out to be an all-lesbian audience. The pay was good at $300 for the weekend. They were nice, but hardly related to my male-female relationship songs. I didn't play there very much.

One of the comics told me about the Laugh-Inn at Garvin's at 2621 Connecticut Avenue, right in the D.C. area. A gentleman by the name of Harry Monocrusos was the owner and booked the talent. He was a very nice guy, and he took a chance on me. I did well and was booked many times, which helped with my relationship — although it did eventually take its toll. I would get $250 and food for the weekend, but had to pay my train fare out of that, so in order to save money, I would have to take the four and a half hour Amtrak instead of the three hour Metroliner. This was an exhausting nine hours of traveling any weekend I got an engagement. It was also impossible to be booked regularly because even if I was that good, no one wanted to see you EVERY weekend!

One day, Harry came up with an idea. He knew who my grandfather was and approached me with his concept. He had heard he could actually book Georgie Jessel, and what would I think of being his opening act. I was ecstatic. What a great idea! I told him I was in. Now, Harry had to make the arrangements to fly Jessel and his piano player in from California. It turns out my third cousin, songwriter Henry Tobias, was going to be his accompanist. This is the same Henry Tobias who was one of the two piano players for my grandfather when he made his legendary appearance at Carnegie Hall in 1950. Henry was seventy-five and Jessel was eighty-two.

The date was set for the Halloween weekend — October 31-November 1, 1980. I was very excited about this reunion. I went to the club early to set up and waited for the arrival of Jessel and Tobias. Suddenly, I looked up and saw Henry Tobias pushing a wheelchair with Jessel sitting there. He was in his usual military garb complete with all his medals — he was Mr. Patriotic and always supportive of our country, even though that was a highly unpopular position during the Vietnam War. As he came before me, I introduced myself.

"Hi Georgie. Remember me? My grandfather was Eddie Cantor."

His only response was: "Your grandfather would have hated that beard!"

That was it — my only conversation with him — for the entire weekend. I did well. He fared less well. All in all, it was a strange engagement. I had hoped for more. Seven months later he was dead.

Paul Colby's

OTHER END

Nov 5
RIDERS IN THE SKY

Nov 6 & 7
MORGANA KING
• • •
BRIAN GARI

Nov 10 & 24
GROVER KEMBLE & ZA ZU ZAZ

Nov 11 & 12
JOHN FAHEY
• • •
THE SONG PROJECT

Nov 13 & 14
THE STRANGERS
(Formerly of HARRY CHAPIN BAND)
• • •
KENT KASPER

Nov 15
TAJ MAHAL

Nov 18
ELVIN BISHOP

Nov 27 thru Nov 29
SONNY TERRY & BROWNIE McGHEE
• • •
ERIC BIBB

TALENT SHOWCASE
Every Monday Night

MORGANA KING

Back in 1981, playing Paul Colby's The Other End (a temporary alternate name for the infamous Bitter End) in Greenwich Village was the ultimate gig. I auditioned like all the others, and I passed. I think it was Paul Colby himself who passed me. I was thrilled. I knew I would be the opening act, but I didn't know for whom. I waited anxiously; would it be another singer-songwriter? Probably not. It had to be a good mix — no competition if at all possible. So no chance that I would be working with any of my idols. No Jimmy Webb. No Randy Newman. No Kenny Rankin. It would all be too similar.

Finally, the call came. I would be playing Friday and Saturday evenings, November 6 and 7, the pay was $35 per night and I would be opening for — drum roll, please — Morgana King. Who? Oh yes, a jazz legend. But I wasn't into jazz, so I don't believe I even had one of her records. I shrugged it off and was simply grateful for the exposure.

Friday evening finally arrived, and I picked a potpourri of my songs that would show a good variety and wouldn't last too long. My entire family showed their support and were in the audience. I think I had just broken up with my girlfriend of two years, so this engagement brightened up an otherwise pretty dark time for me.

When I was backstage in the small waiting area getting ready for my "big time" debut, Ms. King walked in. She asked who I was and why I was there. I explained that I was her opening act. She immediately responded with:

"Oh, what do you do? A comedian?"

"No," I replied. "I'm a singer-songwriter."

Well if looks could kill.

"Are you telling me they booked a singer with a singer?"

"Well, yes, Ms. King. But I'm…"

Before I could go any further, she had a mini tantrum. She was truly pissed off. Suddenly, I heard the announcement:

"Ladies and gentlemen, the Other End is proud to present, Brian Gari."

Now, I can't begin to tell you the feeling I had, knowing that the star of the show was ready to hire a hit man to get someone off the bill. I felt horrible. Here was my first major gig, and the main act wanted to kill me. You have to know how nervous I was in the first place, and Ms. King's warm reception was not making my butterflies fly away. I forged ahead. It was the only thing I could do. I gathered up all the confidence I could muster.

I opened with a nice up-tempo number followed by a more mid-tempo tune. I was quite fearful of looking into the audience, despite my family being right up front. However, when I glanced in back of me, I found

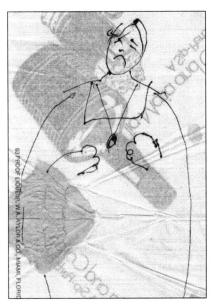

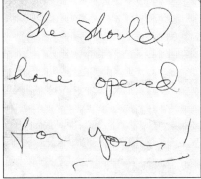

Left: *My father's sketch of Morgana performing that night, which he did on a napkin at the table.* Right: *My sister's note to me while we were watching Morgana's part of the show.*

Ms. King seated in that part of the audience. She wasn't looking as angry. Was I actually winning her over?

I continued with a few words to introduce a little story song, and that got the audience further on my side. I even switched to the guitar from the piano to make sure I showed some versatility. I seemed to be doing quite well, despite all my fears. I talked about the comedy clubs where I had been playing and performed "Late Nite Comic" — long before its Broadway debut. This got a huge response. I looked at Ms. King, who actually seemed to be smiling.

I concluded with "If Our Songs Still Make It (Why Can't We?)," which I wrote about the pop songwriting team of Ellie Greenwich and Jeff Barry. I then took my bows and walked off toward the dressing room — or whatever that little place was called. I was asked to do twenty minutes, and I clocked in at about eighteen. As I passed Ms. King, she looked at me and softly said "Good job." I couldn't believe it. I had actually turned the whole experience around. Morgana King liked me — she really liked me!

A COMIC TRAGEDY
(MARK SENTER)

This story does not center around a celebrity; it centers — no pun intended — around someone who wanted to be a celebrity, but someone who just couldn't.

It was an early night at the Improv in 1983. All of us "borderline" performers were there to see if we could open the show. The word "borderline" is used loosely, as you were only as borderline as an owner made you believe you were. (An owner authorizes the line-up.) Perhaps if a scheduled comic failed to show up, another one would be panting to take his or her place. I was "lucky" — I was a music act; music acts would be the unofficial opener before the first comic. First comics were the ones who would play to the few members of the audience who were there at 9:20 in the evening. This time slot was relished, as it was either this slot or 2 a.m. if you were a rookie. The 2 a.m. slot usually had just as few audience members, but they had the distinction of having consumed about eight times as much liquor by this hour.

At 9 p.m., I was on a bar stool, tuning up my guitar, when in walked Mark — heavy set in his usual polyester navy jacket and striped dress shirt, and smoking that horrendous cigar. Naturally smoke always drifts directly toward those who like it least, as did Mark's.

"Mark," I would say, "how can you smoke that disgusting thing?" He wouldn't say much. What could one say to that question? Apathy was Mark's preference. Had he been another comic, he probably would have joked with, or perhaps even antagonized, me. But not Mark — Mark was used to criticism. He had swallowed a great deal of it being a late-nite act — both from club owners and, of course, the audience.

"You opening tonight, Mark?"

"I don't know," Mark would reply. "I wasn't told for sure."

This usually meant no. Owners often wouldn't arrive until later, making it virtually impossible to make any changes in the first hour's line-up.

"You gonna try Catch?" I'd ask.

"If I can find someone to share a cab uptown with," and with that Mark would shrink away with his near-famous leaning-forward walk. Acts that knew they were doomed for late-nite spots would often hop a cab uptown from the Improv in Hell's Kitchen to Catch a Rising Star, as Catch would start their shows at 9:30 p.m., giving these comics a second chance at going on early.

Comedy had been booming for several years, and more and more clubs had been opening and doing terrific business. (Three clubs in Manhattan, one in Brooklyn, several in New Jersey and Long Island, and, more recently, one on Staten Island.) Comedians could make great money if they maneuvered their bookings well.

Barbara Underhill, former owner of Odds Bodkins on Staten Island, booked me sight unseen. True, I had the Manhattan club credentials, but it does take a brave soul to put new talent on his or her stage. For $20 a night, I'd hop the subway to the south ferry, ride the ferry to Staten Island, and then grab a bus to the club. Quite a journey for that kind of pay, but we performers are a strange breed. We worked for years at the Manhattan clubs for free, until we got smart and upped our price to $5 a show. Ah yes — negotiations this brilliant are observed only at the U.N.

Also trying to save a buck, I asked Barbara who was on the show with me; perhaps I could bum a ride.

"Do you know Mark Senter?" she asked.

"Of course, but I don't have his number."

Mark called me back at midnight. We chatted about how the clubs were screwing us around, but also how we were surviving. I asked him about a ride. Mark explained that although he lived in Queens, he'd be coming from his parents' place on Long Island, so he couldn't help me out.

The line-up for the night was Mark first, me second, and a jazz duo last. The audience was sparse, but there was one large table: a couple of beer chuggers with their women, who also made very admirable attempts at the Heinekens. This, of course, meant trouble — more so for Mark than for anyone else. No emcee was designated, so Mark went up unannounced — a rather unfortunate beginning. The beer guzzlers went at him almost immediately. It was disastrous. He never had a chance. His humor was mostly self-deprecating, and these people ate him up alive. He couldn't tell one joke without an interruption or an insult. If the owner offended them by asking them to be quiet, she might well have lost her only audience. So the war continued — except that Mark wouldn't return the fire. He simply accepted it. Most comics would have either fought or walked. Mark did his time, and I had to follow this — again with no real introduction. Mark left the battlefield and disappeared into the night. That was the last time I saw him — the cigar, the leaning-forward walk, the navy blue polyester jacket.

It was a rainy Saturday in the city when the phone rang. The voice on the other end was my comedian friend D.F. Sweedler. He asked if I had heard about Mark Senter: he committed suicide last Tuesday. There was no humor in D.F.'s delivery.

Footnote: I have since learned that the owner of a very popular club on Long Island was trying to reach Mark a few days before his death. He had a good booking for Mark, but was only getting his answering machine. He never left messages as he had hoped to tell Mark the good news directly.

MARVIN HAMLISCH
AND MIA FARROW

It was 1983, and I was very, very sad. The girl of my dreams, with two children, couldn't make the commitment after our whirlwind affair in New York and South Lake Tahoe. She was scared — understandably so, knowing her ex-husband, the cop. My cat of almost eighteen years had just died as well. The comedy clubs weren't using music acts anymore, and the music business had basically moved to the West Coast, leaving diehard New Yorkers like me in the dust.

I would stare out my window day after day, becoming increasingly despondent; I knew I had to do something. The video world had more than doubled in size, and there were now rental stores everywhere. I found myself renting questionable videos on a regular basis at a store across town that had a good stock of questionable videos — if you catch my drift. The store was called Video Shack and they were backed by (who else?) the mob and had a major interest in pornography with a side of manufacturing. Their stores in Manhattan included one on 49th and Broadway and one on Lexington and Eighty-Eighth Street. I found this one to be the most convenient, as they could also order from the bigger store on Forty-Ninth Street.

I got to know the manager, Chris. She was a nice girl in her twenties — with no ass. Yes, as George Carlin used to say, "Hey — where your ass at?" She knew me as a regular, and after a while she asked if I'd like to work there. I was stunned. Should I really do this?

"You can take home four videos a night," she added. That clinched the deal. I took it part time. I figured it would be safe, as it was not in midtown where anyone would discover me. I didn't want people to see me as a failed songwriter; it was simply a job to keep me sane. I'd be less depressed and make money as well.

On my first day at the new job, who should walk in the door but Clive Davis — the LAST person I wanted to run into at this job. I jumped behind the counter, while the other employees stared at me like I was insane. I whispered to them that he was a major honcho in the music biz and I didn't want him to see me. They understood.

Next, Robert Lansing came in. He was wearing an ostentatious fur coat, and his wife was by his side. I think they had a place on Park Avenue, a block away. Running into him didn't matter as much. He had no idea who I was.

My hours were either 10 a.m.-2 p.m. or 2 p.m.-6 p.m. One of my favorite parts of the job was when the assistant manager, Lance, would send me to the bank and then bring him back lunch from Burger King. Why my favorite? Because at the time, Burger King had a deal; bring us $2 worth of pennies and we'll give you a free Whopper. So what did I do? I went to the bank, dropped off the Video Shack deposit, asked for 200 pennies — in exchange for my two bills — went to Burger King, ate my free Whopper, got Lance's lunch, and came back an hour later. Sometimes I even got on my bike, dropped off my songs to producers in midtown and hurried back. Occasionally, they'd ask what took so long, and I just said the lines at the bank were enormous.

One of the other perks I discovered was delivering tapes to prominent customers. There was this big wig named Carter Something, who would ask that his tapes be delivered directly to him. I took the job because it got me out of the store. What I didn't know about the delivery to this man was that he would give me a $10 or $20 bill every time I got there. Wow! I asked for this job all the time, until I was off one day, and the other employee got the job. From that point on, it was slim pickins for deliveries by me to Mr. Carter.

One day, Marvin Hamlisch walked in. I couldn't escape in time. I actually knew Marvin from years before when he was going with Carole Bayer Sager. He lived on Park Avenue and was going with Cyndy Garvey at that time. She had two little girls, and Marvin came in to purchase some videos for the kids to enjoy on Christmas. He was very nice and acknowledged me in a very kind way. We chatted a bit, and he asked to buy *The Black Stallion*.

We had a racket in the store of taking the rental tapes and re-shrink-wrapping them if a customer wanted to purchase the tape (for a whopping $79.99). I found the last copy of the tape and sold it to Marvin. A week or so later, I was on vacation and called the store to check in. Lance answered and said all hell broke loose with Hamlisch.

"What happened?" I asked completely bewildered.

"The tape was a wood…ock" Lance answered. I didn't understand.

"*Woodstock*?" I asked.

"No, a wood block" Lance exclaimed.

It turns out that whoever re-wrapped that *Black Stallion* tape replaced the actual tape with a black painted piece of wood to make it look like a videotape, so they could sell and/or duplicate it. Hamlisch was furious. I could just imagine him trying to impress those young girls with this big movie and the little girls yelling, "Uncle Marvin, it's a wood block!"

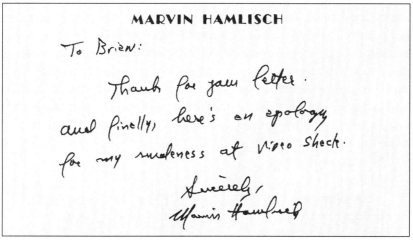

Above: *With Marvin in 2009.* Below: *An apology from Marvin…a few decades later.*

Marvin and I laughed about it many years later. He was a nice man, and his passing is a great loss.

I also had a lot of fun there with the older ladies. All the porno tapes were on display in a secluded room in the back. The men gravitated to it, but there were women who were interested in it as well — long before *Fifty Shades of Grey*. But they needed to be escorted. And who got the job? The manager felt it should be the resident expert, and that could only be me. The ladies would ask for something a little spicy, so I would give them a tape that was really out there. When they would return the next day, they would say that it had been quite an experience. It was hilarious.

One day, the phone rang, and I would always love answering it. It kept me away from the sales, although I was very good at selling tapes.

The lady on the other end said, "Hello, this is Mia Farrow and I'm looking for a certain cartoon for my children."

I wasn't the least bit surprised that it was really Mia. I could just tell.

"Which film, Ms. Farrow?" I politely asked.

"*Dumbo*," she replied.

"Oh, I'm so sorry, that isn't out yet."

"Oh, darn," Mia replied, "is there no possibility of getting it?"

Well, I myself being the collector that I am, had a beautiful copy — on Beta. I told her I had the film, but it was illegal to duplicate. She begged me to help her. I casually mentioned I had heard she sang some of Jimmy Webb's songs for the animated film *The Last Unicorn*. She said she had and even had a cassette — which I could have if I wanted! I said that I could come over with my giant, heavy Betamax and make her a copy of *Dumbo* on VHS for her. She was thrilled. She gave me her address — which was her mother's (the actress Maureen O'Sullivan) — and I took a cab the following Saturday evening — did I mention I had no life? — to a beautiful apartment house on Central Park West. She had just gone out for a date with Woody Allen — his picture with her was in a frame on her bureau. She had left me a note with a bottle of wine and the cassette.

The note read:

For Brian — the rehearsal track. Truely (sic) dreadful. But an exchange of a kind. Gratefully yours, M. Farrow P.S. I hope you like wine....this is a nice one.

Do I still have the cassette? Of course I do! Do I still have the wine? Guess.

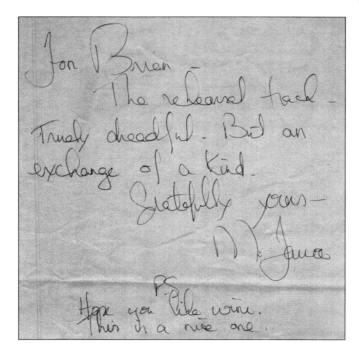

My job did not last. I was asked to clean the toilets one day, as it was supposed to be a shared job among employees. I protested, saying I was only there part time and didn't feel the necessity for this demeaning job, especially since my time on the floor was much more advantageous to them with my selling ability and knowledge of films. They didn't care. I was fired. I went home and cleaned my own toilet.

DAVID CASSIDY

When my father lived on West Fifty-Second Street in his one room with the bathroom down the hall, he rarely had guests. Of course, my mother stayed over when they were dating in the late '40s. My father was an actor/dancer in many Broadway shows during this time, so he also became friends with others in his chosen profession. One such actor/singer was a very handsome Irish American named Jack Cassidy.

Jack was seven years younger than my father and had begun his career on the stage in 1943, in the chorus of *Something For the Boys*. He was extremely charming to members of both sexes. There was no doubt of his talent, but his charm was also very persuasive to not only the ladies but also to anyone who might be able to help him in the industry. It got him ahead and it got him into trouble.

Jack Cassidy and my mother, circa 1950.

One time, when he was drinking a bit too much (he was an alcoholic), he pounded on my father's door in the rooming house and asked if he could stay over. It was not a pleasant evening, as Jack proceeded to get very sick from all the liquor. Despite all this, my father and he remained friends throughout their lives.

When Jack married Evelyn Ward on June 28, 1948, my parents — who had not yet married themselves — were in attendance. Jack was already cheating on Evelyn, so when the pastor asked, "Should anyone here present know of any reason that this couple should not be joined in holy matrimony, speak now or forever hold your peace," there were little chuckles that spread throughout the church.

Out of that union came the birth of David on April 12, 1950. The marriage lasted until 1956; Evelyn had had enough by then and ended up supporting David on her own. She was a beautiful woman who not only performed on Broadway but was also in many television shows.

David and I knew each other in those days and had a lot of fun together as kids. I remember those times fondly. I followed his career from Broadway shows like *The Fig Leaves Are Falling* in 1969 (with a great score by Allan Sherman and Albert Hague) to episodic TV like *Adam-12* and *Marcus Welby*. He had moved to Los Angeles, and I didn't see him at that point.

Meanwhile, Jack married Shirley Jones in 1956 — yes, the same year he and Evelyn were divorced — and they became the couple about town. I recall Jack and Shirley coming by for dinner when we had moved to West End Avenue in 1964. They were both charismatic and fun to be with. My parents also stayed in touch with Evelyn.

In 1970, David auditioned for a cutesy television series called *The Partridge Family*. Ironically, so did Shirley. They both got the parts. Unfortunately, though Shirley was David's stepmother, most viewers believed it was his real mother. That did not sit well with Evelyn — especially because many people involved with the show preferred it that way.

The show made David a bubblegum superstar, and it had him singing songs that appealed to the teenyboppers, but not so much to young people my age. In fact, not so much to David himself. It was kind of an embarrassment for him to be singing some of those songs, most of which didn't impress me either.

Evelyn encouraged me to make contact with David when I made my 1971 trip to L.A. I did, and he invited me over.

It was a far cry from our days in the amusement parks. David had someone named Sam staying with him in his very nice house in Los Angeles. Though still friendly, David and I didn't spend much time there, and I went on to try to make my own name on the Los Angeles music scene. I didn't even bother to approach David with recording any of my songs.

When *The Partridge Family* went off the air in the mid-1970s, David and I were in touch once again. His father had died a horrible death in his West Hollywood apartment, a short distance from where I had stayed in 1971; a fire that was started from his smoldering cigarette when he fell

David and his mom.

asleep on his couch, claimed his life. This incredibly handsome man was unrecognizable, lying on the floor. It was only his ring that identified him. My father was shocked at his untimely passing. In fact, the paintings of my father's that Jack bought went up in the flames as well.

This time, David came to my apartment in New York, and he was quite different from the last time I had seen him. While still fun, things were a little weirder. Yes, we exchanged songs. I played him my new compositions, and he seemed very much impressed. David also banged — and I mean banged — on my console piano by the window. He played so hard, I seem to remember one of the keys being permanently indented! I was not pleased. I think the song was "Darlin" by the Beach Boys. Do I still have that piano? Of course, I do!

He also went into my bathroom and came out with my blue plastic hand mirror. I had no idea what he was doing, but the razor scratched up my mirror and left this annoying white residue all over it. Do I still have that mirror? No! And the residue is gone as well!

I saw him again when he was in town to do *Joseph and the Amazing Technicolor Dreamcoat.* He was very nice to me and whomever I was dating when we went to see him.

The last time I saw him was when he was doing *Blood Brothers* on Broadway in the mid-1990s. His acting was excellent. His mother, my mother, and I all met him at the Michelangelo Hotel (formerly the Taft.) We all had a snack and a drink after David's show; it was the first time I ever got to taste an after dinner liqueur called Limoncello. It was delicious!

David has always been nice to me; when I had my second musical performed entitled *A Hard Time To Be Single*, David couldn't make the show, but he sent signed photos to the cast. For one person in the cast, Larry Victor, it really made his day. He had admired David for years, so this personally inscribed photo had a very special meaning for him, especially when he knew he didn't have long to live. Larry died shortly thereafter from AIDS at age thirty-two.

A few years later, Evelyn starred in my mother's musical *Such a Pretty Face.* (She was even featured on the cover of the CD, which is still in print.) David came to the show and told my mother he was very proud of his mom.

Sadly, the last decade was not kind to Evelyn. At eighty-nine, she was living with Alzheimer's and couldn't walk or talk, eventually succumbing to the disease on December 23, 2012. She had disappeared from our lives and so had David.

STEPHEN SONDHEIM

It was November of 1985, and I was riding my bike down Broadway when I came upon a musical theater legend just standing in front of Lincoln Center. It was the supreme songwriter Stephen Sondheim. I had just been listening to the cast album of his *Sweeney Todd*, and I actually had a question about the lyrics. Did I have the balls to ask him? Yep.

I backed up my bike until I was directly in front of him.

"Steve," I yelled out. He looked over and smiled. "I love your work and have a huge collection, but I have a question about a rhyme in *Sweeney Todd*. I believe there was a false rhyme in one song."

He looked at me curiously. It was shop talk, and he seemed to enjoy it rather than take offense.

"Which song?" he asked.

"I can't recall at the moment, but I think it was a plural…an 's' added to a word, which would technically make it a false rhyme," I replied.

"Can you send me a letter?" he queried again.

"Sure," I responded.

I didn't need to ask for his address. Most people in the business knew of the townhouse where he lived — on the East Side, here in the city. I wrote the letter as soon as I got home. I found the rhyme that the character, Mrs. Lovett (Angela Lansbury) sings:

> *Next week, so I'm told*
> *Beadle isn't bad till you smell it*
> *And notice how well it's*
> *Been greased*
> *Stick to priest*

'Smell it' and 'well it' is a true rhyme but when you replace the word 'it' with the contraction of the word 'it's,' it creates a false rhyme. This is what I wrote to Sondheim; I felt a bit apprehensive, but firm in the facts. What was I in for? Not to worry. Here was the response, on November 14, 1985:

STEPHEN SONDHEIM

November 14, 1985

Dear Brian —

I'm much relieved: you tell me I was
rhyming a plural with a singular. Rhyming
a contraction is another matter, although I
think of it as the last resort. I find it
legitimate because the ear supplies the missing
word and makes allowances for the implied gap.
In fact, I always asked Angie to make a slight
skip between the "t" and the "s". There's a more
egregious example in "Finishing The Hat". But, as
I say, I only use this technique when I can't think
of any other and I don't want to sacrifice the thought.

Thanks for noticing.

Best,

Dear Brian —

I'm much relieved: you tell me I was rhyming a plural with a singular. Rhyming a contraction is another matter, although I think of it as the last resort. I find it legitimate because the ear supplies the missing word and makes allowances for the implied gap. In fact, I always asked Angie to make a slight skip between the "t" and the "s". There's a more egregious example in "Finishing The Hat". But, as I say, I only use this technique when I can't think of any other and I don't want to sacrifice the thought.

Thanks for noticing.

Best,
Steve Sondheim

It was typed and signed by him on his stationery, no secretary involved. What a thrill!

I wrote him back and thanked him for the explanation. Although I must say, some friends told me it was a total cop out — it was still a false rhyme!

I also asked him about a video I wanted so badly. One of my favorite shows of his was *Company*. There was a wonderful documentary made by the great filmmaker D.A. Pennebaker, which documented the making of the cast album of that show. It ended with a chilling finale of Elaine Stritch desperately trying to complete her vocal on "Ladies Who Lunch." I inquired about my ever getting to see it again.

Imagine my surprise when a package arrived in the mail. It was a Betamax copy of not only the film that I wanted but also several other Sondheim rarities that were never released to the home market. Keep in mind, he recorded the tape at the Beta 3 speed, making the quality very dubious. In fact, he included a handwritten note that read: "Sorry about the quality — They're dupes of dupes of dupes of..."

We corresponded on and off for a while after that. He was a generous man.

Note: Starting in the year 2000, Original Cast Album: Company, A Film By D.A. Pennebaker has since been released on Beta, VHS, Laser, and DVD.

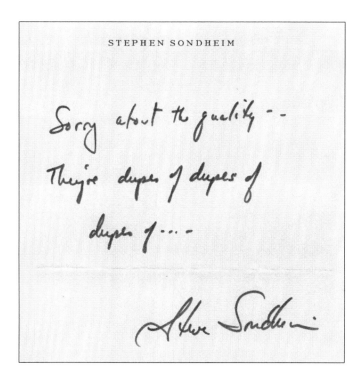

CHRIS ROCK

During the year 1986, I would from time to time still play the comedy clubs, doing my music as an opening or main act. I recall running into this really good comic who wasn't getting booked as he should. He was only twenty-one at the time, and his name was Chris Rock. I found him really funny, despite the many curse words he used throughout his act. He was heavily influenced by his idol at the time, Eddie Murphy. In fact, I wouldn't be surprised if we had both played out at the Rainy Nighthouse in Queens, where Eddie Murphy started. It was really inconvenient to get to, but hell, they paid us. (Although I seem to remember a booking or two when they gave us a hard time.) That was one club where I knew I was doomed because my unknown songs were not of any interest to the rough audience that heckled the comics they paid to see!

Anyway, I also had taken on another job — booking entertainers for a cable TV show. The host was a young guy who worshipped Sinatra and sang Frank's hits on every show. Sometimes I would play for him, but mostly I did my own songs, co-hosted, and sat on the couch with the guests I booked.

He would often ask me to book a comic, but only if he was "clean" — no dirty words on this high class show. I had booked comics like Brett Butler before she hit it big with her own series *Grace Under Fire*. We laughed about it years later at the Westway Diner on Ninth Avenue and Forty-Fourth Street around the corner from the Improv. "That guy hated me!" Brett confided in me in one of the booths, when remembering the response she got, or didn't get, from the emcee.

So I told the host about Chris, and he emphasized once again — no obscenities. I called Chris and told him I wanted to book him for the show. He was really happy, as it seemed this was his first time on TV. I made it very clear that he had a good spot on the show, but there was to be no cursing at all. Could he do that? He said yes.

On January 22, 1987, just two weeks shy of his twenty-second birthday, Chris Rock was scheduled for the live broadcast. It was a snowy night in New York, and Chris was wearing a white sweater and blue jeans. He opened with this:

> *"Was driving down Park Avenue the other day. Saw a prostitute. Asked her how much. She said '$300 I'll do anything you want.' I said 'Bitch, paint my house.'"*

Chris making his TV debut.

Well, that started it. Keep in mind, there was no studio audience, which accounted for the lack of response to any of the jokes Chris would tell. I certainly laughed out loud, as did the few techs, but that didn't quite make up for the mostly major silence. He continued with his act.

"Big issue now. Prison overcrowding. Who gives a fuck."

I looked at the host and he was definitely not happy. He was really pissed. At the end of the six-minute comedy act, Chris left the stage, knowing he messed up. They dubbed in pre-recorded applause.

"Chris will be right here in just a moment." The commercial came and went, but Chris never returned.

Funny thing is, years later, when Chris hit it big, that clip was aired on *Real TV*, *Road To Fame*, *Before They Were Stars*, and *Hard Copy*. The pissed-off host made a few bucks off that "dirty young man."

RICHARD (AND KAREN) CARPENTER

It was the mid-1980s, and I was lying on the floor of my music room, covered by hundreds of audio tapes. My wife at the time, Darla, walked in and exclaimed, "Oh my God — what is all this???" The songwriter Jimmy Webb knew I was an expert on his music and decided to hire me to archive and annotate all his miscellaneous tapes featuring his music.

He was working with the late producer-choreographer Michael Bennett at the time. Bennett provided him with office space at his 890 Broadway facilities. I was there quite a bit and eventually picked up all these tapes and brought them back to my place to listen to and preserve. At the end of the project, Webb had beautifully annotated archival reel-to-reel tapes of all his work. He placed them on shelves in his office. I was quite proud of that.

While I was transferring these delicate tapes, I came across one five-inch white box that simply had the name Karen Carpenter on it. I assumed this was just a copy of one of their hits, so I didn't get too excited. However, when I heard the first notes, I began to get goose bumps. It was Karen singing a rare song of Jimmy's, entitled "One of the Nicer Things." This was followed by three more tunes, including the Beatles "Nowhere Man," one by Richard, and one by the late legendary West Coast session man (later of Bread) Larry Knechtel. I looked up these songs, and they weren't on any album. I decided I would reach out to Richard Carpenter, as I knew he was always archiving the work of the Carpenters.

Somehow, I found a direct address for Richard and wrote to him of my find. It wasn't long before I got a call. It was Richard himself!

Brian, you have no idea what you found! This session was the first one that Karen and I ever did [probably late 1968.] It was recorded in Joe Osborn's garage for his Magic Lamp label BEFORE we ever got on A&M. [Joe Osborn was the brilliant bass player on virtually any records that came out of the West Coast, including Jimmy Webb and, of course, the Carpenters.] What you don't know, Brian, is that you are holding

121

the only existing copy of that session! The tapes burned in a fire in Joe's garage. Would you be kind enough to send me that tape?

"I would be happy to make a copy, Richard," I replied, "but this tape belongs to Jimmy Webb, and if I lose it, I'm sunk."

Don't worry, Brian. I will have it sent by FedEx out here and returned right back to you. A&M has the latest transfer facilities, and I want to make a DAT [digital audio tape] at their studios direct from your original source. Please trust me. I will definitely get it back to you. I will send you a little present if you can do that.

What could I do? I knew this was important, so I followed Richard's instructions and sent off the tape. I only hoped Jimmy did not want his tapes right back.

A week or so later, a package arrived at my door. It was the original Karen Carpenter tape and a cassette with a typed and signed note attached:

Dear Brian,
Enclosed please find the "demo" tape as well as the additional recordings we had talked about. I thank you once again for bringing the "demo" to my attention and for entrusting it with me.

Regards,
Richard

P.S. The Karen/Ella medley is from our ABC TV Special Music, Music, Music of 1980. It dawned on me after our conversation that the correct title of Knechtel's tune is "A Different Time."

Richard and I have stayed in touch a bit, but the rare material has remained unreleased to this day.

RICHARD CARPENTER

Dear Brian,

Enclosed please find the "demo" tape as well as the additional recordings we had talked about. I thank you once again for bringing the "demo" to my attention and for entrusting it with me.

Regards,

Richard C

P.S. The Karen/Ella medley is from our ABC TV Special "Music, Music, Music" of 1980. It dawned on me after our conversation that the correct title of Knechtel's tune is "A Different Time."

ANTHONY NEWLEY

It was August 12, 1987, and I was in the throes of my musical coming to Broadway. However, I couldn't pass up an offer of accompanying a Broadway — and all around entertainment — legend.

Anthony Newley was one of my true idols. He came to America in 1962, with a hit show entitled *Stop the World I Want To Get Off*, which yielded hit songs like "Gonna Build a Mountain," "Once In a Lifetime," and the standard "What Kind of Fool Am I?" If the songs weren't enough, he also co-wrote the entire show and starred in it.

He followed that production up with *Roar of the Greasepaint The Smell of the Crowd*, which produced even more smashes. How could you resist songs like "Nothing Can Stop Me Now," "Feeling Good," "A Wonderful Day Like Today," "The Joker," "Look At That Face," and the hit ballad "Who Can I Turn To?" These songs were either constantly playing in my house or even sung by my father.

I was thrilled to get the call from WNBC's Alan Colmes — who is also my longtime friend — albeit the night before the show. I scrambled to make sure I knew all of Newley's songs in his keys. One song that wasn't a hit I decided to learn because I simply loved it. It was one of his more pop-flavored tunes and a song I was hoping he would want to do — if he sang at all on the show. (Remember, he wasn't there to do a concert!) It was my job to make the performer feel comfortable enough to sing, after we struck up a conversation in the green room.

Newley was as nice as he appeared on television. He was incredibly open and kind. He was also very encouraging to me upon hearing that I had a musical coming to Broadway. He had worked with our leading lady, Teresa Tracy, so he was even more enthusiastic.

During the show, Alan opened up the phone lines, and Newley took some calls. One caller turned out to be my sister, who told him of her role as Evie in a college production of *Stop the World*. He was so gracious, and he was excited to know my sister won Best Actress for her part in the show.

Besides being willing to do any song we asked for — in lower keys because, as he put it, "everything is a little lower now" — he also was totally amazed when I mentioned that obscure song that I liked so much. "Lunch With a Friend" turned out to be one of his all-time favorites as well, and he was thrilled to do the song with just me on the piano! I had printed out the words, in case it was a little too obscure for him to remember.

He actually told the story of how he wrote it — both musically and lyrically. It seems he never played an instrument and depended on musical

Newley and me outside Alan's studio. August 12, 1987.

arranger Ian Fraser to understand his chord ideas. The lyric was based on a true story, which absolutely fascinated me. A good friend of his and his wife's came on to his wife. This disappointed him tremendously and inspired the song. So we did the number "live" on the radio, and he was most pleased. The phones lit up, and Newley, Colmes, and I had a great time.

Upon leaving the studio, Newley insisted we stay in touch. He gave me his private address and phone number and wished me luck once again on my musical. (I needed more than that!)

We corresponded for the next several years; he told me he was going to be doing *Stop the World* again in London, so "I won't be seeing him hanging around the drugstore for a while."

On May 1, 1996, I planned an early Mother's Day surprise for my mother. I found out Newley — HER favorite performer as well — was going to be playing Rainbow & Stars here in New York's Rockefeller Center. She had no idea where I was bringing her that night. I think I even turned down the place card on our table, which had his picture on it, in order to keep the surprise a surprise until the moment he arrived on stage. It was thrilling to watch her reaction — as well as being a thrill to watch Newley stroll out. It was a great show, and I got to introduce her to him afterward.

He lived less than three years after that, succumbing to renal cancer at only sixty-seven years old. It has been said that his medical care was not very good and that he should have survived. He really should have — he was such a sweet man.

GEORGE CARLIN

I had been a fan of George Carlin's since his "straight" days, when he was wearing a suit and tie and appearing on numerous variety shows in the mid-1960s. I even had his first album for RCA entitled *Take-Offs and Put-Ons*. Both my father and I marveled at the incredible comedic mind of this man, long before he became the favored comedian of the hippie generation.

In 1971, my father and I learned that George would be performing in Greenwich Village at the Bitter End. He had just tried out his new material at a little place called The Focus Coffee House at 163 West Seventy-Fourth Street. His next stop would be The Bitter End.

We had no idea this would be a groundbreaking appearance; we had expected the usual George doing his TV bits like The Hippy Dippy Weather Man. We were astounded at what we were seeing. This was a whole new George Carlin — and a great one at that. We had an incredible time. We had just witnessed what was to become a comedy legend.

I followed George's career by owning every comedy album he released, as well as taping every TV show he was on from the time I bought my first Betamax in 1977. He was my comedy hero.

It was natural for me to include his name in a lyric I wrote for the opening number of my Broadway musical, *Late Nite Comic*, in 1987. The male lead was a piano bar player with aspirations of being a comedian. I came up with "I'm through playing Harold Arlen...I'll be the next George Carlin."

When the album came out in July of 1988, I carried around copies with me just in case I ran into someone who might be able to give it some exposure.

On November 17, 1988, I made great use of one of those albums. As I was leaving a friend's office at CBS on Sixth Avenue and Fifty-Second Street, who should I run into on my moped but George Carlin! He was on his way down Sixth to do *Late Night With David Letterman* at NBC. I shouted to him that not only was I a major fan but I also had all his early records and TV appearances. He was extremely gracious, but in a rush to get to the show. I thanked him for all the laughs, and I drove down Fifty-Third Street toward Seventh Avenue. I suddenly realized I should have given him an album. With that thought in mind, I sped down Seventh, turned left on Fifty-Second Street again and caught up with him.

"I'd like you to have my album of a Broadway show for which I wrote the score," I blurted out.

"Is this your address?" he asked as he pointed to the back of the album.

"Yes," I replied.

"I'll definitely write you, Brian," he said.

We both sped off to our mutual destinations.

I then recalled that I had his name in the opening song. Would he actually take the album back to California with him? Would he really sit down and listen to it?

A few weeks later, I got a huge package in the mail with George's return address on it. I thought he was probably returning my album. I couldn't have been more wrong.

Not only did he send me his latest album autographed by him but he also included a video I had wanted, as well as a rare 1964 audio tape. And if that wasn't enough, there was a handwritten note from him that read:

> *Brian,*
>   *I enjoyed the show album very much. I wish I could have seen the show.*
>   *Your music is great. It's my first 'mention' in a lyric.*
>
> *Thanks,*
> *George*

Do I still have that note? Of course I do!

On May 31, 1990, Regis Philbin announced that George Carlin would be on the show the next day. I decided that night to compose a letter that would show Regis what a great guy George was. Unfortunately, I waited 'til it was rather late in the evening to drop it off to Regis's apartment building. The next morning I tuned into the show, and while George was sitting there, I see Regis reaching into his pocket. It was my letter.

REGIS: *Doorbell rings. By messenger. 10:30 at night. Guy says "Dear Regis — I'm sure you already know what a fine person George Carlin is, but I thought you might be interested in what happened to me. Last year I spotted him rushing down Sixth Avenue to get to a David Letterman taping. Even though he was in a hurry, he took the time to say hello. I told him of my rather large George Carlin collection and of a few missing items. He took my address and told me he'd be in touch. To my surprise a few weeks later, not only did he personally write back, he sent a package of all my missing Carlin stuff. A rare human being."* Nice letter.

george carlin

Brian,

I enjoyed the show-album very much. I wish I could have seen the show. Your music is great. It's my first "mention" in a lyric. Thanks.

George sat there on the stool, grinning as he recalled our encounter. He simply responded to Regis with "Right. Good. Sure. Yeah. That's nice." Like that's how you treat your fellow human beings.

On May 14, 2006, the New York Times ran a piece on me called "Through the Glass Brightly." It was written by John Freeman Gill and concerned my intense interest in old New York and especially the Upper West Side. It got a huge response, but nothing surprised me more than an e-mail on June 25 from my old friend George Carlin. I couldn't believe it. He was writing ME! Seems George still got the New York Times delivered to him even in Venice, California.

BRIAN:

    I SAW THE NY TIMES ARTICLE IN MAY. I'D LOVE TO TALK ABOUT NY EXTERIORS.

    THEY ARE ALSO A PASSION OF MINE, ALTHOUGH ON A MUCH LESS ORGANIZED, LESS-INFORMED MANNER THAN YOURS.

    I'D LOVE TO LEARN MORE.

GEORGE C.

George always typed in caps.

It turns out that George was as enthralled with Upper West Side history as I. I forgot for a moment how logical that would be, given his growing up in Morningside Heights — or should I refer to it as George did: White Harlem. He had a great fondness for his old neighborhood, and whenever he came back to town, he would visit. His last love, Sally, told me of some of their wonderful times in the old "hood" during their years together. George made it clear that he wanted to get together with me at my apartment when he was going to be back in town. He was fascinated by my collection of photos and video. He wrote me another e-mail on July 13.

> BRIAN:
>
> I'LL BE IN NEW YORK 7/19 — 7/29. I'LL BE WORKING, BUT I HAVE THREE FREE DAYS: 24, 25, 26. MAYBE WE CAN GET TOGETHER. I'LL BE AT THE RIHGA ROYAL ON 54TH STREET:
>
> STAY COOL,
> BIG GEO FROM THE COAST
>
> PS: BESIDES COVERING "WEST-SIDE NEW YORK" STUFF, I WANT TO ASK YOU SOME THINGS ABOUT MY CAREER ARTIFACTS.

George ended up booked on one show or another, and our visit never happened.

He was the only one other than family who had my cell number.

One time, I was sitting in the airport and my cell phone rang. I looked at the number and it was from California. I decided to answer. It was George.

"Hey Brian, I'm trying to find out the name of this guy on Ed Sullivan who had an act with a dog that didn't do any of things he was asked to do. I thought you'd probably know the answer."

"Well, I wish I could give you the answer, George, but right now I'm sitting in an airport."

"Oh, that's okay. I'll figure it out somehow. Talk to you soon."

I turned to the woman I was with and said, "That was George Carlin. He called me to ask me a question. I can't believe it." I called my father and a million friends. "George Carlin just called me."

George and I got even closer with e-mail. He sent me a couple of audios that were hysterical. One was a phony phone call about prison sex that turned out to be Wanda Sykes, and another was the clock lady that aired on Howard Stern.

From May 4, 2007, (after the publication of my first book "We Bombed In New London"):

YOUR BOOK. SOMEHOW, IT GOT LOST IN THE SHUFFLE OF CHANGING ASSISTANTS; MOVING OUT OFFICES; MOVING MY RESI-DENCE; BEING IN THE HOSPITAL TWICE FOR HEART FAILURE;

THE GOOD NEWS? I JUST PUT YOUR BOOK IN MY AMAZON SHOPPING CART.

LOVE FROM THE COAST,
BIG GEO

From December 13, 2007:

BRIAN:

AS I FEARED, YOUR FIRST MAILING OF YOUR BOOK WAS HOPE-LESSLY BURIED UNDER A REALLY BIG MESS THAT WAS DUMPED IN MY LAP (AND MY NEW ASSISTANT'S LAP)

AS A RESULT OF FIRST, MOVING OFFICE LOCATIONS, AND SECOND, CHANGING ASSISTANTS.

MY APOLOGIES TO YOU.

I NOW CAN READ IT TWICE.

THE BIG DVD COLLECTION OF HBO SHOWS WILL BE MAILED SOME TIME NEXT WEEK,

SEE YA;
GEORGE

From December 30, 2007, after sending him my Twentieth Anniversary CD of Late Nite Comic:

GARI

YES, I GOT THE ORIGINAL CAST CD. THANK YOU FOR THAT. I'LL BE PUTTING IT IN MY I-TUNES LIBRARY SOON.

AND I ALSO GOT THE THANK YOU. I HOPE YOU ENJOY SOME OF THE OLDER SHOWS. ALTHOUGH THE LATEST WORK IS THE BEST.

GEO
PS — — — I'M NOTORIOUSLY LATE WITH E-MAILS.

He once again called me to ask if I would be willing to organize his storage unit. Despite my overwhelming desire, I had to admit that a local West Coast resident would be a better choice. I gave him my friend

Kenny's number. He said he would make certain that I would get something great from that storage unit.

I invited him to the October 2008, Friends of Old Time Radio Convention, where we would have honored him. This was his response on May 6, 2008:

BRIAN:

THANKS FOR YOUR KIND SUGGESTION. IT SOUNDS LIKE FUN, BUT, I REALLY KEEP THINGS LIKE THAT AT ARM'S LENGTH.

I KEEP OUTSIDE ACTIVITIES AT A MINIMUM, BECAUSE MY WRITING AND PERFORMING OCCUPY ALL MY ATTENTION, AND THEY KEEP ME VERY HAPPY AND SATISFIED.

ONE NOTABLE EXCEPTION: THIS THURSDAY NIGHT THE PALEY CENTER FOR MEDIA (FORMERLY THE MUSEUM OF TELEVISION AND RADIO) IS HONORING ME WITH AN EVENING. THE FUNNY PART IS, IT'S THE THIRD TIME THEY'VE DONE IT: ONCE IN NEW YORK, NOW TWICE IN L.A. THE GOOD THING IS ALL I HAVE TO DO IS ANSWER QUESTIONS AND TAKE COMPLIMENTS.

NO EFFORT. I LIKE THAT.

BUT THANKS AGAIN, YOU'RE A GOOD FRIEND. AND DON'T FORGET, I'M GOING TO FIND A SPECIAL PIECE OF MEMORABILIA FOR YOU WHEN I FINALLY HAVE THE TIME AND COURAGE TO WADE INTO THE STORAGE BIN.

BEST,

GEORGE

That piece of memorabilia was never to arrive; George died on June 22, 2008 — exactly five months to the day after my father's death.

DOC POMUS
AND PHIL SPECTOR

When I was about fifteen, I opened up the Manhattan phone book to see if a legendary songwriter by the name of Doc Pomus was listed. He was. He had written iconic songs like "This Magic Moment," "A Teenager In Love," "Viva Las Vegas," and my personal favorite, "Can't Get Used To Losing You." This represents only a tiny portion of his hit catalog.

I called him at his home at 888 Eighth Avenue in the heart of the music district in Manhattan. It was a stone's throw away from the Brill Building, where he wrote so many of his hits. He was incredibly gracious and receptive. We hit it off, even though he was almost thirty years my senior. He told me great tales of the music business that no one else was privy to. He liked to go to Fascination, a part of an arcade up the block on Broadway, when Broadway had fun places with brightly lit games in the '60s. I joined him from time to time. He was part of my life through my high school graduation, my first love affair, my marriage, my divorce, and my Broadway show.

Doc moved up to 253 West Seventy-Second Street in the '70s; it is the same building where the Goodbar murder took place, and Doc even knew the victim. In spring of 1976, my first love was living across the street from Doc, and he would often see her on the block. Of course, I would always want to know if she would consider coming back. Doc was direct — sometimes in a not so delicate way.

"It's over, Brian. She ain't coming back. Get over it. It's finished."

His response did not please me to say the least. It simply broke my heart even more. But Doc wasn't always like that. He also was very kind and considerate and would call me for no other reason than just to stay in touch. We even wrote a song together.

Doc started having annual birthday parties to which I was always invited. He had interesting guests at this open house affair on Seventy-Second Street. The door to apartment 1107 would literally be open, as icon after icon jammed into Doc's two rooms. Everyone from John Belushi to the legendary blues singer (and Doc's idol) Joe Turner could be seen enjoying Popeye's Fried Chicken — courtesy of my brother-in-law, who ran the site up the block from Doc's apartment. Doc would be holding court in the middle of the festivities, dressed in his extra-large red shiny shirt.

One such occasion was particularly special, a shared event with his famous lawyer brother, Raoul Felder. It took place at 8 p.m. on Wednesday,

June 13, 1990, at Katz's delicatessen on the Lower East Side. The food was incredible — how could it not be? It was a deli!

Once again, the celebs were all over the party, and this time it included friends of his well-known brother. As I wandered through the crowd, I happened to see one of the all-time greatest rock and roll producers: Phil Spector. Spector was an old friend of Doc's, as Doc was like a father and mentor to him. Doc knew Spector was eccentric, but it didn't change the dynamics of their close relationship. Doc never stood for bullshit and would make sure you knew that.

As I got closer to Spector, I observed him seated next to a guy I knew — a rock journalist who was the biggest bore on the planet. I don't know what it is about certain writers who write about pop music, but a lot of them are the most dreary, excruciatingly dull people I have ever met. You would think the excitement of the music would be reflected in their personalities; not so — at least in this case.

At first, I was disappointed seeing them together, feeling I would not have my chance at a conversation with Spector. I didn't have to wait long for that to change. I could see Spector's body language. He was squirming and trying to subtly get away from this pain-in-the-ass. Finally, in not such a subtle manner, Spector got up and walked away from this guy. It was hysterical. The guy was left with egg on his face. Spector had no interest in him. I, on the other hand, felt I had a lot to talk about with Phil, and I decided I would take my shot.

I approached Phil and immediately started talking about some of the more obscure songs I knew he produced. I also mentioned some of his lesser-known writers that I had admired so much. Suddenly, Spector had

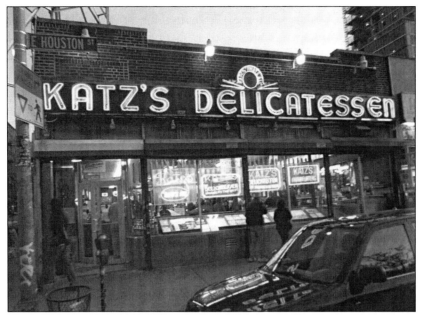

Katz's Delicatessen.

At the Pomus birthday bash in back of Doc with Paul Shaffer at far right and Doc's brother, Raoul, at the cake.

an interest in speaking with me. We chatted for quite a while. I couldn't believe I was having this intense conversation with one of rock's most controversial producers. He liked me — he really liked me. (Sorry, I think I used that one before.)

As the repartee wound down, I noticed his lapel button. It was red and said "Back to Mono" in white letters. This was a phrase he was known for,

Phil's pin.

since he always liked his records better in mono. This was because with stereo, you had two channels, and that could change the dynamics of how you would listen: mono mixes created only one way to listen. Phil made up buttons that reflected this personal preference, but I only saw them on his jackets. I got up the courage to ask him a question.

"Is there any chance you might be able to get me one of those buttons?" I innocently asked.

Without missing a beat, Spector took the button from his lapel and gave it to me. In total shock, I thanked him as he got up to leave. Do I still have that button? Of course I do!

Doc, a four-pack-a-day smoker for decades, but who had given it up, contracted lung cancer a short time after this last birthday celebration. He died the following year. The funeral was on March 17, 1991, at Riverside Memorial Chapel and was attended by many of Doc's close friends and associates, including Spector, who flew in from his home in California.

It would have disappointed Doc greatly if he had lived to see Spector get indicted for the death of actress Lana Clarkson. I certainly had mixed feelings for Phil; he was so nice to me in those fleeting moments at the party, but how can you admire a man when you know of the horrendous death of this beautiful woman at his hands?

GERALD MARKS
AND IRVING CAESAR

Here are two songwriters from the Tin Pan Alley era. Gerald Marks could always be seen walking along West Fifty-Seventh Street, where he lived. You couldn't mistake that tall, bald gentleman with those giant black-rimmed glasses. He had co-written the classic "Is It True What They Say About Dixie" and the standard "All of Me."

One time in June of 1994, I walked up to Gerald and introduced myself. I told him of my connection to Eddie Cantor, and he began to tell me this great story about him.

In 1935, when Marks was thirty-five, he worked on a song with Sammy Lerner called "Oh Suzanna (Dust Off That Old Pianna)." Their publisher was the legendary Irving Caesar, who offered to show the song to Eddie Cantor. Of course, that made Caesar feel he was entitled to a cut of the writer's percentage of the song — not just the publishing. Oh well, they say fifty percent of something is better than one hundred percent of nothing.

So Caesar called my grandfather, and Marks went over to play the new song for him. If he liked it, the tune would end up on his top-rated radio show and sell a ton of sheet music. Well, Marks played the song for him and didn't get much of a response. He went home to his apartment at the Dorilton on Seventy-First Street and Broadway, feeling very dejected.

The next day, at six in the morning, the phone rang. Being a songwriter, Marks usually didn't get up until noon. This phone call was insanity to him — until he heard Cantor's voice on the other end.

"Could you come over to my apartment here at the San Remo on Seventy-Fifth Street and Central Park West?" Cantor queried. "I want to learn that cute new tune you played for me yesterday; I'll have some bacon and eggs ready for you."

Bacon and eggs was not appealing to Marks at this hour, but he splashed some water on his face and rushed over to play the song for Eddie Cantor, who planned to sing it that very night.

It turned out to be a big hit not only that night but for several shows afterward. Strangely, Cantor never recorded it, but I did put it on a CD entitled *The Show That Never Aired* — a radio show that never got on the air because it was pre-empted by President Roosevelt. I presented it to Mr. Marks, which pleased him greatly.

I loved Marks. He was a sweet guy and once performed at my mother's

Gerald Marks posing in front of my mother's house, 1994.

apartment for all the Eddie Cantor Appreciation Society members. He lived until ninety-six, passing away in 1997. I was lucky to have met him and to hear that story, which would have gone with him to his grave.

Irving Caesar was another legend of the Tin Pan Alley Broadway scene. He had offices forever in the Brill Building until he finally moved his files to 850 Seventh Avenue, and then to his apartment in the Omni Park Central Hotel (formerly the Park Sheraton.) This landmark hotel housed Jackie Gleason's offices in the '50s and was the last place Fatty Arbuckle slept.

You might not know his name instantly, but you would surely know his classic lyrics like "Tea For Two" and "Swanee." He was also the inspiration for Martin Short's character Irving Cohen ("Give me a bouncing C").

He had horrible eyesight and donned coke-bottle glasses his entire life. You couldn't miss him in the theater district, usually standing on the corner of Fifty-Fourth Street and Seventh Avenue. I kept seeing him and decided to say hello. He was pleased, and in the early '90s invited me to visit him in his office above Smiler's Deli. I agreed.

His office was like a trip back to the days of Cantor, Crosby, and Jolson. Chipped sheet music of his hits were up on the walls in cheap frames all over his tiny office. I wandered about and helped him preserve some of

In Irving's apartment, 1992.

the rare films he owned, which I'd discovered lying in a corner. I had them duplicated by a friend. Do I still have them? Of course, I do!

Irving had a lady named Bertha, who helped him for decades. She was a kindhearted old woman, who welcomed me into the office.

Eventually, I was invited to his apartment in the hotel, which was a block away, on February 26, 1992. I decided to bring my video camera as he was now ninety-five and might not have much time left. Bertha has passed away, and now there was a much younger lady named Chris, who guided me into his apartment, sixteen floors above Seventh Avenue. She knew a lot about him — a lot about his income especially.

The reason for my visit was not only to say hello again but also to give him a copy of a previously unreleased Cantor recording of a song he had written. "It Goes Like This (That Funny Melody)" was recorded for Victor in 1928. Caesar had written it with Cliff Friend, but although others had recorded it, Cantor's rendition had been held back. While working on a Cantor project for RCA, I found it, put it out, and made a copy for Caesar. A big smile came over his severely wrinkled face while listening to it on a little cassette machine. There he was in his red bow tie, gray sweater, and moccasins, enjoying his little tune for the first time — at least this version. He spoke so highly of my grandfather, and he told me of his collaborations with George Gershwin. He also told me where he wrote some of the biggest songs of the twentieth century. We chatted about his growing up on the Lower East Side of Manhattan at 106 Ludlow Street — now gone.

The last time I visited him, Chris had moved him into a swanky apartment house on East Fifty-Second Street. Gone were the dark, dingy surroundings that Irving called home for so many years. The new place worked very nicely for Chris, I am sure.

His songs brought in millions. He had no relatives or immediate survivors. Irving lived 'til 101 — probably a lot longer than Chris thought he would, when she somehow got him to marry her. She became his beneficiary and inherited all his copyrights. The Songwriters Hall of Fame and ASCAP tried to intervene. I don't think it worked. She was Mrs. Irving Caesar by law.

KATHARINE HEPBURN

My dear friend, the late composer-pianist Arthur Siegel, played on all the Ben Bagley-produced albums that featured theater composers. These albums included many guest stars, one of whom was Katharine Hepburn. Arthur and Kate grew close in around 1990, when they worked on the *Cole Porter Revisited album Volume IV*.

In the early '90s, Arthur had been diagnosed as a diabetic. During one hospital stay, he was actually visited by Ms. Hepburn, which absolutely thrilled him. Imagine knowing this immense star cared enough to come to your hospital room. I certainly was impressed.

I was even more impressed when I saw the documentary about her on PBS entitled *All About Me*. She was about eighty-six at this time and just as beautiful and sharp as she was in her prime. It made me think about how great it would be to end up with a woman like this. So much so, that I decided to let Ms. Hepburn herself know my feelings.

I asked Arthur for her address and told him I wanted to write her a nice note. He thought it was sweet and gave me her contact information. I didn't write some long fan letter; what I wrote was this, in the spring of 1994:

Dear Ms. Hepburn:

I am a friend of Arthur Siegel's and I just wanted to let you know that I hope I meet a woman with your beauty and your intelligence one day and that she continues to be as beautiful as you are at your age.

Fondly,
Brian Gari

On April 7, 1994, I received an answer on a card with the name Katharine Houghton Hepburn embossed at the top. The date was actually written as IV-7-1994.

Katharine Houghton Hepburn

IV - 7 - 1994

Dear Brian Gari -

    I hope for your sake - that

she has all the good qualities and

none of the bad - Good luck -

I was absolutely floored. What an honor to get such a personalized response typed and signed by her. But the story doesn't stop here.

I had a recording studio in those days, and I put impressive correspondence and photos up on the walls. This, of course, qualified. So I found a little frame and hung it prominently in the room for all to see. You wouldn't think that would be a problem for anyone. Well, I guess it was.

About once a week, the framed letter was knocked to the ground. I couldn't understand why. The nail was strong. I decided to keep an eye on it whenever people were booked to record.

One day, a composer who wrote a very famous TV theme was there with his partner, recording again. He had been there several times. I looked up to find the letter knocked to the ground again. I confronted this guy.

It seems he thought this was an actress who was actually related to Ms. Hepburn and who had an extremely similar name — and he hated her. They had some kind of a run-in, and he never wanted to see a reference to her again. Holding back my anger, I responded that this wasn't his property, and it was from Ms. Hepburn herself — not any relative. He sheepishly said he was sorry, and I don't think I ever saw him again. Do I still have that letter and is it still up on the wall? Of course it is!

JERRY STILLER

Around September of 1997, someone alerted me to that month's issue of Vanity Fair. They said I should read the page on Jerry Stiller: "he mentions your grandfather." I was excited by the connection of Eddie Cantor and Jerry, because Jerry was a current major star, and The Eddie Cantor Appreciation Society (the fan club) was certainly hoping there would be some prominent big names that would want to be associated with our group. We had people like Mel Brooks and Soupy Sales, so Jerry would be a welcome addition.

My connection to Jerry was minor until then. Coincidentally, I had met his daughter, Amy, some years earlier, and we had one date. She wasn't very interested, even with my singing a little song I wrote for her into her phone machine. It was not to be.

The Vanity Fair article had a question: "Which historical figure do you most identify with?" Jerry's answer was, "Eddie Cantor. He made people laugh during the Depression."

I was incredibly touched. How wonderful that this man would acknowledge my grandfather today. Not many people remembered. Jerry did. I found Jerry's address — he lived only eight blocks from me — and I wrote him a thank you note. I also asked if he would like to join our fan club. I got an immediate response.

"Of course I'd love to be part of The Eddie Cantor Appreciation Society. He is truly one of the greats."

And so began a special friendship. We corresponded for a while, and when his book came out in the fall of 2000, he included a photo of my grandfather — courtesy of yours truly — which had a notation next to it: "I wanted to be funny like him."

When I managed to get my grandfather's autobiographies reprinted in February of 2001, Jerry and Anne were surprise guests at the signing we had at Barnes & Noble. They were so funny and so gracious.

In April of that same year, a frightening time in my life suddenly occurred. It started with a slight backache and turned into agonizing and crippling pain. My parents came by and realized we had to get me

Proust Questionnaire

Jerry Stiller

From his *Ed Sullivan Show* days to his current success as Frank Costanza on *Seinfeld*, Jerry Stiller has proved to be the most resilient of comedy stars. This month, he takes five from berating his hapless TV son, George, to star in HBO's *Subway Stories* and to reflect here on the joys of Eddie Cantor, Sherlock Holmes, and raising his real-life showbiz family

Who is your hero in real life?
Barbara Buloff, my therapist.

Who is your favorite hero of fiction?
Sherlock Holmes and Dr. Watson.

Which living person do you most despise?
I'm working on it.

What is your greatest extravagance?
Overtipping the people who love my work.

What is your favorite journey?
Jerusalem. Where it all began.

What do you consider the most overrated virtue?
Saintliness.

On what occasion do you lie?
When telling someone the truth is too painful.

What do you dislike most about your appearance?
No space between my pelvis and floating rib. It's lowered my height.

Which words or phrases do you most overuse?
"Fill me in."

What is your greatest regret?
My mother not seeing my marriage work out and my mother never seeing her grandkids.

When and where were you happiest?
At a screening of *Seize the Day* in the 80s.

What is your greatest fear?
Jerry Stiller without Anne Meara.

What is your idea of perfect happiness?
To continue to perform.

What is your favorite occupation?
Getting paid to act.

What is your most marked characteristic?
Hollering at George Costanza.

What do you consider your greatest achievement?
Marriage and raising a family while having a career.

Which historical figure do you most identify with?
Eddie Cantor. He made people laugh during the Depression.

Which living person do you most admire?
Chuck Feeney, who gave away millions anonymously.

What is your most treasured possession?
My memory.

Where would you like to live?
Where I am right now, but on a higher floor.

What do you most value in your friends?
That they don't take me seriously.

How would you like to die?
Not onstage. It would ruin the show.

If you were to die and come back as a person or thing, what do you think it would be?
A whale.

If you could choose what to come back as, what would it be?
Myself, without baggage.

What is your motto?
Qui s'excuse s'accuse. (He who excuses himself accuses himself.)

FOR DETAILS, SEE CREDITS PAGE

to a hospital. I was taken out of my apartment on a stretcher — knocking down my Eddie Cantor poster while trying to get through my small hallway.

The staff at the hospital diagnosed me with a herniated disc. I was on morphine for days — and that didn't help much. Doctors came and went, but to no avail. Jerry heard about my ordeal and, having had the same problem, sent over his staff with a book on back pain by John Sarno. Finally, I had an epidural that didn't quite cure me, but got me on my feet long enough to get the hell out of that hospital.

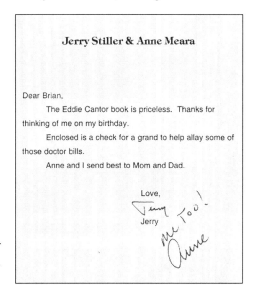

When I got home, the bills arrived promptly. I was pleased I had insurance — or so I thought. It seems that all the years I was paying Blue Cross, the only coverage I had was for the hospital — that didn't include doctors. So I got these whopping bills from them and had no way to pay. Here I was, still crippled by the disc pain, yet having to deal with these immense bills only added to my misery. Word got back to this dear man, Jerry Stiller, and suddenly a check arrived. I was kind of embarrassed, thinking I was now a charity case, but this man's kindness and love for my grandfather dominated any thought of shame I might have had.

> *Dear Brian,*
> *The Eddie Cantor book is priceless. Thanks for thinking of me on my birthday.* [I had gotten him a book.]
> *Enclosed is a check to help allay some of those doctor bills.*
> *Anne and I send our best to Mom and Dad.*
>
> *Love,*
> *Jerry (me too! Anne)*

He saved me.

Jerry with my mother and me at Barnes & Noble, February 26, 2001.

Anne Meara, Jerry Stiller, and me looking thru old photos at Surprise Lake Camp, July 22, 2001.

By July, we all ventured out to the summer camp, Surprise Lake, which was celebrating its 100th birthday. This is a camp where underprivileged children went, including my grandfather. It was a place he supported his entire adult life. Yes, Jerry went there, too, and so did Larry King and Neil Diamond. Located in Cold Spring, New York, the camp gave these kids a breath of fresh air, and so many people have told me of my grandfather's love of that place. Jerry and Anne joked around and gave us many laughs on that outing.

Jerry has continued to support all my ventures, including all Eddie Cantor releases as well as introducing me at Barnes & Noble in January of 2008 — less than a week after my father's passing — for the release of my first book and CD concerning my Broadway show. Oh, and how could I forget the most impressive of all: his appearance at my wedding. Since Eddie Cantor was his idol, he would have been most proud of his number one fan.

ROBERT CLARY

Okay, maybe this chapter doesn't count because he's related to me, but I'm including him anyway. I have known Robert virtually all my life. He arrived in the States from France in 1949 and couldn't even speak English, but he had a hit record, which he learned to sing phonetically. Merv Griffin introduced him to my aunt Natalie, and they were immediately inseparable. They had dinner together every night. She would pick him up from his small apartment in back of Grauman's Chinese Theater in Hollywood — ironically, the same apartment building where I stayed on my first solo trip to Los Angeles in 1969.

Robert went on to star on Broadway in *New Faces of 1952* and was a huge success, leading to major nightclub engagements and more records as well as film, stage, and television. Of course — television. He created the iconic part of Louis LeBeau in the 1965 hit series *Hogan's Heroes*. It was at this time that he became my uncle. Yes, he married my aunt Natalie in Las Vegas that same year. In fact, the ceremony was taped — and given to the wrong couple, who probably are wondering to this day why they own this tape of an unknown Frenchman saying "I do."

They were living in Natalie's small house on Edris Drive when I came to visit in the summer of 1969 (see the Mystery Man chapter.) I was all of seventeen at the time and Robert wasn't particularly interested in my songwriting plights. In fact, during those years, Robert was making many appearances on television variety shows. He always did songs that were already hits or standards, and I came to accept that it was just the way things were. He didn't take chances.

But things were not going to stay that way forever. In the early '90s I began to take charge of my grandfather's legacy. I created a publishing company where I shared the royalties with my mother and aunts. I did very well for them and was appreciated by most of the family.

Meanwhile, my hard work did not go unnoticed by Robert and Natalie. They were rather amazed at the progress I had made with the releases of my grandfather's work on CD, and later, DVD. Natalie passed away in 1997, and I continued sending Robert my latest Cantor projects.

In June of 2000, I was finally able to get my grandfather's two autobiographies republished. My mother and I did a mini book tour, eventually landing at Barnes & Noble in Los Angeles in March of 2001. Robert supported us by participating in the little talk we had at the signing in the bookstore. We also celebrated his seventy-fifth birthday with him that same month.

Clowning with Merv Griffin when he first arrived in the States. (Check out the feet.)

We were staying with him, and as I was about to leave for the airport, he asked if I'd be interested in reading his memoirs and possibly getting someone interested in publishing them. I said I would, but I also knew how hard it would be for me to find time to read it.

As it turned out, I had to come out to L.A. once again in late May, and I knew I had to read the book before I got there. I decided to take it on

My aunt Natalie with Robert.

the plane with me. I couldn't put it down. There I was with tears rolling down my cheeks as I read page after page of Robert's three years in the concentration camps. It also included great stories about his life in the entertainment world.

My girlfriend at the time had joined me for the trip, and I wasn't quite finished reading the book. She was very understanding as I lay on the bed in Robert's guest room and completed this beautifully written autobiography. I told Robert in no uncertain terms that I would get it published. (I had no idea how, but I was bound and determined.)

When I got back to New York, I immediately called the publisher of the Cantor books, Michael Dorr, and unbeknown to me, he was a big World War II buff, so Robert's book had a double interest to him — the war and entertainment.

The next thing I knew, I had a deal for Robert. I called him immediately, and he was overjoyed. The book came out in the fall of 2001. It was entitled *From the Holocaust To Hogan's Heroes* and has since sold a very good amount of copies, going from hardcover to paperback. It continues to sell.

I have developed a very close relationship with Robert: I've created a web site for him and I answer all his e-mail — of which there is still a substantial amount every week.

One very special thing that came out of the growth of my deep feelings for Robert is a song I wrote after seeing a documentary about him in March of 2000. The 1984 film was called *Memoir Of Liberation A-5714* and it brought me to tears once again. I couldn't stop thinking about it. It finally inspired me to write the following song.

MON ONCLE BORN IN PARIS
HAD A CHILDHOOD OF SPLENDOR
MON ONCLE DIDN'T KNOW A RAINY DAY
HE RAN TO BUY SOME ICE CREAM
EVEN WITH HIS EMPTY POCKETS
MON ONCLE KNEW PAREE WHEN IT WAS GAY
BUT OVERNIGHT HIS FAMILY GREW CONCERNED
WHEN YELLOW STARS WERE EV'RYWHERE YOU TURNED

MON ONCLE LOST HIS FAMILY
AND HIS CHILDHOOD OF SPLENDOR
MON ONCLE SAW THREE YEARS OF RAINY DAYS
AND THRU THE CLOUDS OF DARKNESS
HE WOULD TRY TO FIND SOME SUNLIGHT
HOPING SOMEWHERE HE WOULD SEE SOME SWEET BOUQUETS
BUT FLOWERS DIDN'T BLOOM WHERE HE WOULD PRAY
AND ALL HIS PRAYERS WOULD END UP IN DECAY

MON ONCLE CAME FROM PARIS
AND ARRIVED IN CALIFORNIA
MON ONCLE TOOK AMERICA BY STORM
THE AUDIENCES LOVED HIM
HE WAS BLESSED WITH RECOGNITION
MON ONCLE LOVED TO SING AND TO PERFORM
AND EV'RYONE WAS CAPTURED BY HIS CHARM
BUT NO ONE SAW THE NUMBERS ON HIS ARM

I produced a video to go along with the song and presented it to him at his seventy-fifth birthday. I had written it a year before, so it was very hard for me to keep it a secret and hold it back until his birthday. It was worth it. It has created an even stronger bond between us and is a very beautiful moment every time I come to L.A. and perform the song with Robert in the audience.

Robert and me today.

Gene Baylos on The Hollywood Palace.

GENE BAYLOS

Remember the old time comedians at the Park Sunset I told you about? Well, this concerns one of them: an old Borscht Belt one named Gene Baylos. He was loved by his fellow comedians — known as a comedian's comedian — and had done the *Ed Sullivan Show* as well as *Milton Berle*, *Joey Bishop*, *Dean Martin*, and the *Hollywood Palace*.

Besides filmed comedy shows like *Car 54* and *That Girl*, he also did dramatic shows like *Kojak*.

But he was never a huge success, and he lived with his wife, Cyrile, in their New York City apartment at 310 West Fifty-Sixth Street. He had a corner table at the Friars Club on East Fifty-Fifth Street, where he'd have lunch every day. He'd always bring a sandwich back to a homeless man, and in the winter, he got him a coat. When a friend offered to give the guy some more clothing, Baylos replied "Hey! Get your own bum!"

It was a rather cold day in the '80s, a decade after my meeting Baylos in L.A.; I happened to be driving my motor scooter by Seventh Avenue and Fifty-Fifth Street — right near my mother's apartment — when I saw him again. There he was in his old overcoat, just standing on the corner. I stopped my bike and said, "Hey Gene — remember me? Eddie Cantor's grandson from the Park Sunset Hotel?" He looked at me, and a big smile came over his face. He said "Of course I remember you, kid." We chatted for a while, and I went on my way. I would see him many more times on that same corner, and I'd always say hello. Eventually, I made some connections that got me to the dining room of the Friars Club. It was always a fun time to look around at the tables and see faces of some of the big — and not so big — names of people in show business. Over at table twenty-four I noticed a familiar face; it was Gene. I went over to him, and he replied with the same line, "I remember you, kid." I genuinely liked him, and I guess he liked me too. Maybe I was the son he never had. Maybe it was because I cared enough to acknowledge the older, established comic in my midst.

In November of 2004, my father was recovering from open heart surgery at the Jewish Home For the Aged on West 106th Street, and I found myself wandering the hallways. I noticed a poster on the wall of an evening honoring a resident named Gene Baylos. I asked a nurse if he was indeed there. She showed me to his room. When she introduced me to him, he jolted at me from his bed with a grunt and a growl similar to a ferocious lion that literally knocked me backwards. I was very scared. I left the room immediately. The staff said it was dementia. He was ninety-four and died four years later. He didn't remember me anymore.

LUNCH WITH SOUPY SALES

It was another Saturday afternoon in the winter of 1960, noon to be exact, and I was sitting in front of my aqua — I think it was aqua; I'm color blind — black-and-white television set, ready for my favorite show, *Lunch With Soupy Sales*. All of us eight-year-olds would get our vegetable soup and grilled cheese sandwiches and a glass of milk — sometimes with Flav-R-Straws or maybe Bosco chocolate syrup — and watch this fun and unique comedian/host as he did his famous Soupy shuffle, showed old time movie clips, and reminded us of important sayings — "Be True To Your Teeth and They Won't Be False To You" — on his Words of Wisdom blackboard.

He also cavorted with his two dog characters, White Fang (The Biggest and Meanest Dog in the U-nited States) and Black Tooth (The Sweetest Dog in the Whole Wide World.) The grunting voices were provided by the talented Clyde Adler. Soupy would often go to the door and be met by an irate neighbor, which resulted in some kind of a pun or insane joke. He also introduced puppets such as Pookie the lion, who might lip sync to a hit song of the day. Of course, nothing could beat Soupy getting hit in the face with a pie. We lived for that! Part of the fun would be hearing the laughter from the crew on the set. Kids instinctively knew that others were enjoying it as well, although we never knew what a crew was.

As the years went on and we kids were getting older, Soupy didn't lose touch with his audience. He came along with us. In 1964, when he arrived at Channel 5 in New York City, we were now in our early teens. Soupy was our hero for many reasons. He never talked down to his young viewers and actually made us think he was one of us.

One of the funniest moments at Channel 5 was New Year's Day in 1965, when Soupy told us that we should tiptoe into our parents' bedroom and find our mom's pocketbook and our dad's wallet and take those little green pieces of paper with guys with beards on them and send them in an envelope to him. He would then send us a postcard from Puerto Rico. Well, most of us knew this was a joke, but the few dollars that weren't

Monopoly money were given to charity. Unfortunately, some executives at Channel 5 felt they should suspend him, and that they did. He was back a short time later because all of us protested against the network.

Soupy also created a dance called "The Mouse," which led to a hit record. You couldn't go anywhere in 1965 without either hearing it or doing it. He landed on all the rock and roll shows that we teens enjoyed.

 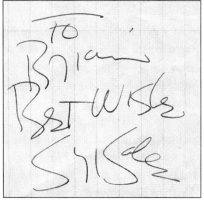

He was even doing "The Mouse" on that famous *Ed Sullivan* show where the Beatles made their debut! I recall meeting him just one time in 1964. I attended all of the game shows that were being produced here in New York. For years, I had forgotten about the show where I got his autograph, which I had kept for close to forty years. Do I still have it? Of course I do!

About ten years ago, I attended a concert of Vince Giordano's Nighthawks, a top notch '30s-style band that has devotees like Mel Brooks, who show up again and again. I looked in back of me, and there was none other than Soupy himself. I said hello and mentioned I had a clip of him, which I had taken with my 8mm camera in 1964. Would he like to have it? He and his beautiful wife, Trudy, were very gracious and gave me their phone number. That started our close friendship. There was never a time that I didn't stop and say to myself, "This is Soupy Sales, my childhood hero and now my friend." Unfortunately, within these two short years, Soupy's health deteriorated until a life threatening heart operation had to be performed. Soupy pulled through. His strength was enormous. Perhaps it was due to the many years of dancing and prat falls, or maybe it was just sheer determination. Or perhaps it was music.

The first music Soupy heard when he came out of heart surgery was that of vibe player Terry Gibbs. It may have actually pulled him through. He would listen to it on a tiny cassette player. I thought to myself, *If only*

Soupy with Terry Gibbs, 2003.

Soupy with Brian, Christmas Eve 2004.

I could bring Terry Gibbs to Soupy in person. A week later, I was reading the New York Times and came across a story that said Terry Gibbs would be performing a concert here the next day. I called all over town and located Mr. Gibbs. I simply asked if he would sign a get well photo to Soupy. He did more than that. He said he would come to the hospital on the way to the airport. I brought along Vince Giordano, who was armed with Terry Gibbs CDs. As we approached Soupy's room, who should be sitting in a wheelchair right behind us but Soupy himself. He was thrilled beyond words. It was lunchtime, and the nurses were bringing in Soupy's sandwich. I was offered one as well, and as I bit into one of the sandwich halves, I realized things had come full circle; I was really having lunch with Soupy Sales.

The last photo session November 9, 2007.

GOODBYE DAD

"Brian, I think you should check on him," Sandy, my father's oldest friend, demanded.

"He's probably fine," I replied.

He was a few weeks shy of his eighty-eighth birthday and had been plagued by health problems, not the least of which had been his heart. He was miserable with his ill-fitting teeth inserted over worn out gums. He was also losing his eyesight. But just a week earlier he was looking incredibly dapper at the Friar's Club *Salute to Comedy* dinner. He was also immensely proud of a modeling job for Esquire Magazine, where he was seen as a wizard with Andy Samberg from *Saturday Night Live*.

My mother, who divorced him forty years earlier — but remained his friend — also attempted to reach him. Only the answering machine came on. She too thought I should check on him. I dreaded this chore. I also knew in my heart that although there had been previous scares that amounted to nothing, there would come a day when it would not be a false alarm.

I drove my motor scooter to his apartment building at 8:30 p.m. and asked the doorman if he had seen him that day. The reply was no.

"How about yesterday?" Negative again. I started to shake as I headed home, five blocks away, for the keys.

Ten minutes later, I was opening up his apartment door. I could see directly into the kitchen, where one light was eerily left on.

I heard his year-old cat scramble in fear.

I saw his body on the floor.

I raced in and softly said, "Dad, Dad," as I touched his head.

His glasses had been thrown a few inches from the refrigerator, where his head was resting. I called 911. They asked if I knew CPR. I said his face was down and his body was stiff. They understood they couldn't help. They sent the police, the medics, and a detective. The detective discovered something.

"Look at this," he exclaimed. He read the beginning of a letter written the day before about his experience on the Esquire shoot. My father's words stopped in mid-sentence.

"I guess he died yesterday," the detective matter of factly summed things up. I picked his glasses up off the floor and put them in my pocket. I was afraid they might break.

I don't know if I told
you. This modeling job
was the horror of all
time. It was way down
on Grant St. Which is
now all Chinese & no one
speaks English. It was a
very cold day plus rain.
I was cast as the "Wizard".
Thank God the costume
was big enough so I
could wear my

Gari and Sandy in NYC, late '40s.

SANDFORD DODY, ROBERTO GARI AND THE CHAIR

Sandford Dody was a close friend; his connection with my family goes all the way back to the '40s on Swing Street (West Fifty-Second Street between Fifth and Sixth Avenues.) He and my father lived at 7 West Fifty-Second Street in a rooming house; my father lived on the second floor, facing the courtyard, while Sandy lived on the fifth (top) floor. Sandy was jealous that my father had a bigger room, but Sandy paid $5 a week for his, and my father paid $7. Chan Richardson, future wife of Charlie Parker, lived with her mother in a cheaply divided room next to my father. The building was razed in 1957 for the huge Tishman office building at 666 Fifth Avenue.

Sandy (as he was known to all of us) was a writer and a bit actor. He had hopes of being a playwright more than anything else and had just missed having his first play produced on Broadway. He had a great sense of humor and became my father's best friend. As bachelors, they would often go to the beach together, comparing tans — no one knew about skin cancer in those days. They would eat in the neighborhood together, although Sandy's enormous appetite and demands for larger portions got them banned from almost all the little eateries up and down Sixth Avenue.

One time, while eating at the Automat, Sandy went to get a piece of pie from behind those little windows that displayed your food; the pie would pop out when you inserted your nickel. But suddenly, ALL of the windows opened! Sandy yelled, "Gari, Gari, come over here!" They ate like kings.

After my father married in 1949, Sandy and he still remained close. My mother would often invite Sandy to dinner at our Upper West Side apartment; he would walk all the way up from Greenwich Village — where he lived — every time, right up until the day he died, after leaving Fifty-Second Street. He was a fun guest, and all of us were charmed by

167

him with his English accent. (When asked about this, he would say he wasn't British — just affected.)

In 1958, Sandy got his first break as an author. He wrote the memoirs of Dagmar Godowsky, and it was quite a success. Unfortunately, Sandy was the ghost writer and got no credit on the cover. It did, however, lead to other contracts, also penned more by Sandy than the celebrities themselves. "The Lonely Life" (Bette Davis) was published in 1962, followed by more autobiographies on Elaine Barrymore (1964), Robert Merrill (1965), and Helen Hayes (1968). He finally wrote his own book, entitled "Giving Up the Ghost," in February of 1980. In that book, he would be quoted as saying, "Is there anything madder than an autobiography written by anyone other than oneself?"

When he began work with Helen Hayes, he called her Miss Hayes and she called him Mr. Dody. He felt this had to stop, so, after working constantly together in her bedroom, he finally said to her "You were great in bed today." From then on they were close friends.

At one point, when Sandy was going into the hospital, he insisted to my father that he would not come out alive. My father told him over and over that he would be fine, but Sandy was morose — so much so that he asked my father what he would like of his.

Sandy said, "You obviously don't need money."

"What? What makes him think I don't need money?" my father said to himself.

Anyway, after constant prodding, my father finally gave in and said he would like the chair Sandy kept near his front door. Sandy said that was fine. A week later, when Sandy left the hospital, he called to say he was okay.

My father's response was, "You gotta be kidding! I rearranged my whole goddamn apartment to accommodate that chair!"

Years later, Sandy came into a lot of money from an inheritance, and he started a tradition of taking my then divorced father to dinner about once a month, in a little village restaurant called Gene's on West Eleventh Street, just a few blocks west of his longtime apartment. After my father died in 2008, Sandy continued the tradition with me. It was sad taking my father's position, but it was good to see Sandy. It didn't last long. Sandy passed away himself on July 4, 2009, at age ninety.

Sandy, Dad and me, October 2006.

INDEX

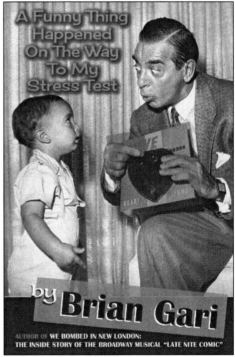

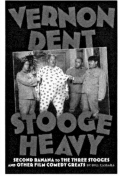
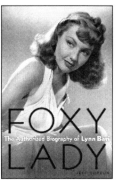